UNDERSTANDING
Tarot

UNDERSTANDING
Tarot

DISCOVER THE TAROT AND FIND OUT WHAT YOUR CARDS REALLY MEAN

LIZ DEAN

CICO BOOKS
LONDON NEW YORK

Please note that Tarot cards are intended to be treated responsibly and with respect. Generally, they are not suitable for children. The way one reads Tarot cards may be guided by the information in this book, but ultimately the interpretation of the cards is up to the individual, for which neither the publisher nor author can be held accountable.

This edition published in 2019 by CICO Books
an imprint of Ryland Peters & Small Ltd

20–21 Jockey's Fields   341 E 116th St
London WC1R 4BW   New York, NY 10029

www.rylandpeters.com

First published in 2003 as *The Mystery of Tarot*

10 9 8 7 6 5 4 3

Text © Liz Dean 2003, 2019
Design © CICO Books 2003, 2019
For picture credits, see page 156

A CIP catalog record for this book is available from the Library of Congress and the British Library.

ISBN: 978-1-78249-725-7

Printed in China

Designed by David Fordham
Edited by Mandy Greenfield

CONTENTS

INTRODUCTION

The TAROT IS A STORY, as all good mysteries are. Its reputation has the romance of the Romanies, the power of the Italian dukes who commissioned the first cards, and a 600-year-long popularity. One episode saw the cards being carried by persecuted missionaries as a secret code; another twist had the Tarot denounced by the Church as "the devil's picture book." Yet universally the Tarot has been a tool for those seeking enlightenment.

There is no end to the Tarot saga, for whenever the cards are consulted and laid out in a spread, a new story begins. The narrative is never fixed, because the events revealed in a reading reflect the nature of our own thoughts and actions, which constantly change. The cards themselves do not create events; they reflect key issues in our lives, empowering our future choices.

ABOVE: *The Sun, from* The Classic Tarot, *1835. The engravings are by the Italian artist Carlo Della Rocca.*

Learning Tarot is like learning a language, but it uses symbols as a way to explain itself. The occultist A. E. Waite, in his *Pictorial Key to the Tarot*, says: "Given the inward meaning of its emblems, [the cards] do become a kind of alphabet which is capable of indefinite combinations and makes true sense in all."

It is hoped that this book inspires you to learn how to use the Tarot and benefit from the insight that this ancient mirror of life provides.

How to Use This Book

The first and second chapters present a history of Tarot cards and their symbols. It suggests the threads of their mystery, from what are possibly the oldest surviving cards—the fifteenth-century Visconti-Sforza—to the evolution of the esoteric decks created from the 1700s onward. At this time, connections between the kabbala (an ancient Jewish mystical tradition) and astrology were established, and these are also examined in this section.

The third chapter shows you how to lay out the cards for a reading, ranging from the simplest three-card spread to more detailed layouts, such as the Celtic Cross and the Tree of Life. There are examples of genuine readings to demonstrate how the cards work in action, and how they relate to—and illuminate—each other during interpretation.

Chapter Four offers interpretations for all seventy-eight cards: the twenty-two cards of the major arcana and the fifty-six of the minor arcana. For the major arcana there is a passage on the card's symbolism, and another that decodes the astrological symbols that appear on many Tarot decks. The historical deck shown is the Visconti-Sforza Tarot; the modern deck is *The Magic of Tarot* deck (see page 155 for

ABOVE: *Some Tarot decks are inspired by the work of well-known artists, such as the Giotti and Salvador Dali Tarots. The card above is from* The Dante Tarot, *created by Andrea Serio.*

further details). Each interpretation presents card combinations and some include a historical anecdote, so that you can see how specific cards work in conjunction with one

another, or delve deeper into the origins of salient cards.

The card interpretations for the minor arcana are grouped by their number and type, each with an introduction explaining their numerology. Learning the card numerologies can be a valuable shortcut when reading the numbered (or "pip") cards, particularly if your deck has geometric designs rather than illustrated pips. The Court card introductions help explain how these cards act as energies, as well as representing specific people; for the beginner, the Court cards can be notoriously difficult to relate to, if they are considered solely as personalities.

Turn to page 155, Tarot Resources, for recommended Tarot "bibles," the authors of which I thank here for making the deeper study of this subject, and its practice, so rich and enjoyable.

1 Tarot Traditions
Court and Clergy: Europe's First Tarot

Pagan, Egyptian, kabbalistic, early Christian, satanic: these terms have all been used to describe the ancient system of divination that is Tarot. Yet these descriptions really relate to the user more than they do to the cards themselves. This can be seen in the myriad decks that are available today: there is the Arthurian Tarot and the Tarot of the Witches; the Salvador Dali deck and the Jung-based Mythic Tarot; the Tantra, Ukiyoe, and Game of Thrones Tarots; the Tarot of the Sphinx, Tarot of the Cat People, Motherpeace Tarot, and Aleister Crowley's Thoth Tarot; along with numerous astrological Tarots, fairy Tarots, love Tarots, and I Ching cards. All seek to explain the mystery of Tarot through a host of broader cultural and individual belief systems.

The earliest Tarot decks appear to have been commemorative paintings commissioned by royal families, yet, by the nineteenth century, the Tarot had become a treasury of occult wisdom. So what happened in the intervening centuries to change Tarot from courtly art to high magic?

It is thought that Tarot cards were originally designed for sole use at the royal courts of Europe, for games and divination. In 1392, a painter named Jacquemin Gringonneur was commissioned to paint three packs of richly decorated cards, "ornamented with many devices," for Charles VI of France. His fee was

Above: *Justice from the Charles VI (Gringonneur) deck originally dated as 1392, although it is highly likely that these cards are of fifteenth-century origin.*

ABOVE: *The High Priestess, or Papess, of the Visconti-Sforza deck. The Visconti family had her painted in the likeness of their ancestor, Sister Manfreda, who was a member of a religious sect who had elected her as Papess.*

entered into the court treasurer's ledger, which was once considered the first documented evidence of decks of Tarot cards in Europe. Seventeen cards supposedly from this deck, previously known as the Gringonneur or Charles VI deck, are preserved at the Bibliothèque Nationale, Paris. However, it is unlikely that these cards are the Gringonneur ones—scholars believe they were painted in Ferrara in northern Italy in the late fifteenth century. One clue to this lies in the style of armor worn by the Page of Swords, which is of a later design more consistent with the fifteenth than fourteenth century. This Ferrara deck is now known as the Estensi, after the dynastic D'Este family who commissioned them, and it's assumed that the Gringonneur actually referred to a deck of playing cards, rather than the first Tarot.

Italian courts were commissioning Tarot cards as early as 1415, when a deck—the Visconti Tarot—was painted for the Duke of Milan, probably by the artist Bonifacio Bembo. Its successor, the Visconti-Sforza Tarot (see page 155) is believed to be the oldest Tarot in existence.

The Visconti-Sforza Tarot is thought to have been created to commemorate the marriage of Bianca-Maria Visconti to Francesco Sforza in 1441. The marriage represented the alliance of two of the most powerful families in northern Italy, and the deck reflects the early tradition of exquisite, hand-painted cards, which often carried the family insignia. The Ace of Staves (Wands) of the Visconti-Sforza Tarot is inscribed with the motto "A bon droyt"—which is variously translated as "with good reason" or "the right path." The deck, in structure and imagery, was the forerunner of the seventy-eight card deck we know today.

In Italy, the term Venetian or Piedmontese is used to refer to decks of seventy-eight cards, as opposed to decks such as the ninety-seven-card Florentine pack (known as a *minchiate*) and the Bolognese pack, which comprises sixty-two cards.

TAROT AS TRADE

LE · MAT

THE INVENTION OF WOODBLOCK PRINTING in Germany in the fourteenth century marked the beginning of mass production and the rise in popularity of playing cards and Tarot cards among ordinary people. By the mid-1400s, card-making workshops were flourishing in Italy, France, Germany, and Belgium, and card-painting soon became a specialized trade acknowledged by craftsmen's guilds. Religious opposition to Tarot cards, and the banning of foreign imports (whether playing cards or Tarot decks), reveals their prevalence, popularity, and economic viability at this time. In the mid-fifteenth century a Franciscan friar preached a sermon in northern Italy condemning dice and Tarot cards, and the Church referred to Tarot cards as "the devil's picture book," which may have been part of an agenda to suppress the philosophy of Gnosticism throughout Europe. Gnostics (from the Greek word *gnosis*, meaning "knowledge") believed in esoteric wisdom, which the Church deemed heretical (see page 12).

ABOVE: *In woodblock printing, the outlines of the card images were printed, and then the colors were stenciled or hand-painted. The Marseilles deck is an example of this production method; its design was based on earlier Tarot styles.* Tarot of Marseilles *was published in 1701–15 by the artist Jean Dodal. Later decks were painted by Nicolas Conver, master papermaker at Marseilles in 1761.*

WHERE DID THE NAME TAROT COME FROM?

The multitude of theories about the origin of the word Tarot reflects the debate surrounding the true origin of the cards themselves. There is little factual evidence to support any of these claims—only the interpretations of Tarot historians and occultists.

The simplest explanation is that the word Tarot is a diminutive of *tarocchi*, an Italian card game from which Tarot developed. The cards may have been named after the River Taro in the plains of northern Italy, where the oldest surviving decks were painted. The French *les tarot* and German *tarock* may be derivatives of *tarocchi*.

Tarot scholar Dr Yoav Ben-Dov (1957–2016) suggests Tarot derives from the Italian word *taroccho*, meaning "Fool" or "dumb person" in colloquial sixteenth-century Italian. Given the Tarot deck has one Fool card, *taroccho* may have meant "the Fool's deck."

Then there are the esoteric theories: "Tarot" stems from the Egyptian word *Ta-rosh*, meaning "the royal way," associating the cards with the pharaohs of Egypt as both earthly and divine kings. Tarot may be a part-anagram of the Latin word *rota*, meaning "wheel" (*rota* appears on the Rider Waite Smith Wheel of Fortune card). Or, according to the magician Aleister Crowley (1875–1947), Tarot came from Torah, Hebrew for "the law," so aligning the Tarot with kabbala, the Jewish mystical system.

ABOVE: *The Crocodile, or Fool, from the* Grand Tarot Belline, *a nineteenth-century French deck conceived by one psychic, Magus Edmond, and published by another, Magus Belline. The card's interpretation may translate as: "All kinds of misfortune threaten you. There is nothing to fear, as you only have to wait for salvation from heaven."*

KNIGHTS AND GYPSIES

SOME PEOPLE BELIEVE THAT THE ROMA (ROMANIES), OR "GYPSIES," brought Tarot cards to Europe and that the word "gypsy" is a corruption of "Egyptian," derived from Little Egypt (Epirus), a region of Peloponnesia in Greece; another theory suggests the Roma originally came from India. There is no evidence that they invented the Tarot; however, it is more likely that they brought Tarot cards or playing cards to Europe as they emigrated west during the 1400s.

The idea of Tarot may have been already familiar to medieval Europeans before the 1400s: in a sermon in Switzerland in 1377, the German monk Brother Johannes Rheinfelden described the rules of a card game and how it offered moral guidance for people of all walks of life.

Gnostic sects in Europe may have used Tarot cards to teach the illiterate their belief in Dualism, which is the interplay of opposites. These opposites—male and female, darkness and light, death and rebirth—are common themes in the Tarot. In this way, Tarot themes and archetypes were perhaps used for instructional rather than divinatory purposes. The Waldenses, a Christian dissident sect founded by Peter Waldo in 1170, may have used the cards as a secret code. The sect was banned by the Church, but thrived in secret, so Waldensian missionaries traveled throughout Italy (often in disguise) seeking converts. Known as *barbe*, or uncles, they would dress as tradesmen to ensure their safe passage. The Magician card may have represented a

ABOVE: *The Knight of Wands from the* IJJ Swiss Tarot *is dressed cavalier-style, his red tunic symbolizing the energy of the suit.*

barb in disguise, since in early decks the Magician is shown as a cobbler. Roger Tilley, in his book *The History of Playing Cards*, proposes that the Magician card may have been used by Waldensians as a passport to identify themselves to other devotees. In France, the Magician has been titled "Le Jongleur," the juggler or minstrel—a wandering bard.

ABOVE: *The Knight of Cups from the Visconti-Sforza deck. A graceful youth on horseback holds the chalice, his suit symbol. His graceful offering may be at odds with the more forceful energy generally associated with the knights.*

The Knights Templar, an ascetic military order, has also been associated with Tarot cards. The order was founded by Hugh de Payens of Burgundy and Godeffroi de St Omer, a French knight, in 1119. Their mission was to protect pilgrims and the routes to the Holy Land. Over time, the order became rich and successful.

As its influence grew, the Knights became a target for persecution by the Church, which sought to stamp out the many unorthodox sects operating at the time. Philip IV of France charged the Knights with heresy; they were arrested and their possessions seized. Their grand master, Jacques de Molay, was burned at the stake in 1314. Again, there is no documented evidence to tie the Knights Templar in with the Tarot—however, a cross appearing on the Ace of Coins cards in the French Vieville pack has been identified as the Templars' insignia.

CAVALIER·D'ÉPÉE

ABOVE: *The Knight of Swords from the* Tarot of Marseilles. *The Knights denote action and in Tarot are often indicators of events speeding up.*

THE ORIGINS OF THE MINOR ARCANA

ABOVE: *The Ace of Swords, shown with a crown and decorative fronds, is from the* Liguria-Piedmont Tarot, *published in 1860. The style of this deck shows the fusion of both Italian and French Tarot traditions.*

THE TAROT IS MADE UP of twenty-two major arcana cards, or trumps (triumphs), and fifty-six minor arcana cards, which are divided into four suits. This being so, it seems likely that these arcanas may have existed separately and were combined to form the complete seventy-eight-card deck at a later stage. The minor arcana originated from playing cards thought to have come from eleventh-century China and Korea, where sets with four suits were in use at court. Early decks from southern China often have the suits Coins, Strings of Coins, Myriads of Strings, and Tens of Myriads—the forerunners of Hearts, Spades, Clubs, and Diamonds of our modern playing cards. In medieval Italy, merchants plied the trade routes from Venice to the Orient, so it is quite likely that the card-painters of northern Italy were exposed to, and influenced by, Oriental card systems.

The Italian author Giovanni di Covelluzzo, writing in 1480, had yet another theory, but little evidence. He believed that playing cards were introduced into Italy in 1379 from Arabic North Africa. If this happened at all, it is more likely that the minor arcana reached Italy from North Africa via Spain, which was Arab-occupied until 1492. In Spain, these cards are known as *naipes;* when they appeared in Italy, they were known by their Saracen name, *naib.*

ABOVE: *The Ace of Cups, c. fifteenth-century Italy, shows a central chalice with a double-arced fountain. An arrow appears where the two streams of water divide, with a sword to the right and an anchor to the left.*

THE LEGEND OF THE GRAIL

The legend of the Holy Grail provides another mysterious link to the possible origin of the minor arcana cards. The Four Grail Hallows were the grail itself, or the chalice used by Christ at the Last Supper; the sword used by King David in the Old Testament; the sacred lance that pierced Christ's side during his crucifixion; and the platter that held the Passover lamb.

Perhaps the best-known example of the grail stories in medieval England is *Morte D'Arthur*, a compilation of grail legends written by the English knight Sir Thomas Malory. Published in 1485, it is likely that Malory's work was based partly on the earlier work of Chrétien de Troyes in the late 1100s. De Troyes, a French writer, penned Arthurian romances for his many wealthy patrons to satisfy their curiosity about British mythology after the Norman Conquest. He, in turn, was inspired by Celtic mythology.

The Irish predecessors of the Four Grail Hallows were the Four Treasures of Ireland: the Cauldron of the Dagda, the Spear of Lug, the Sword of Nuada, and the Stone of Fa. Many contemporary Tarot packs draw on these legends and name their minor arcana suits after the treasures. The Cauldron equates to Cups, the Spear of Lug to Wands, the Sword of Nuada to Swords, and the Stone of Fa to Pentacles. The

Arthurian Tarot uses the characters and sacred objects of the grail legend in its major arcana. Card I, the Magician, is Merlin; the High Priestess is the Lady of the Lake; the Emperor is King Arthur; and the Wheel of Fortune is the Round Table.

THE FOUR SUITS OF VISHNU

The Hindu creator-god, Vishnu, may be another potential answer to part of the Tarot mystery. The four suits of the minor arcana are symbolized by his four arms, in which he holds four sacred objects, some of which correspond directly to the emblems of the suits. He holds the disk, for preservation (Pentacles); and the club, for wisdom (Wands). The third object is the lotus, for love; associated with femininity, the lotus may link with the suit of Cups. The conch, for inner realization, does not at first glance sit well with the remaining suit of Swords. However, in Hindu tradition the conch was used to sound the war-cry before battle, so it may imply the martial nature of Swords after all.

THE OCCULT REVIVAL: EGYPTOMANIA

ABOVE: *This modern Egyptian Tarot, painted on papyrus by Silvana Alasia, was partly influenced by the Tarot created by the late nineteenth-century occultist Jean-Baptiste Pitois, a follower of Eliphas Lévi (see opposite).*

THE LATE EIGHTEENTH and early nineteenth century saw an occult revival. Many of the associations made with the Tarot at this time have influenced modern thinking on the card meanings. Up to this point, there had been no obvious link between the Tarot and Egypt or kabbala.

The landmark text of the occult revival was authored by French esotericist Antoine Court de Gebelin. In his treatise *Monde primitif* of 1781, de Gebelin claimed that the Tarot itself was actually an ancient Egyptian book containing secret wisdom. This was the Book of Thoth, named after the Egyptian god of healing, wisdom, and the occult.

After de Gebelin's death in 1784, a Parisian barber and wigmaker (or merchant, according to some sources) Jean-Baptiste Alliette, continued his work. Under the chosen name Etteilla—Alliette spelled backward—he wrote esoteric books, worked as a fortune teller, and produced his own Etteilla Tarot deck. He claimed that in this deck he had restored the ancient Egyptian designs. He also included the Tarot's links with kabbala, the mystical tradition that originated in Judaism (see page 24). When Napoleon invaded Egypt in 1798, Egyptomania reigned; as artifacts raided from tombs and temples found their way to Europe, the work of de Gebelin and Etteilla gained credence and popularity.

ABOVE: *The Moon from* The Tarot of the Sphinx, *by Silvana Alasia. In this modern deck, two Anubis dogs replace the dogs or wolves seen on the Rider Waite Smith deck (see page 18).*

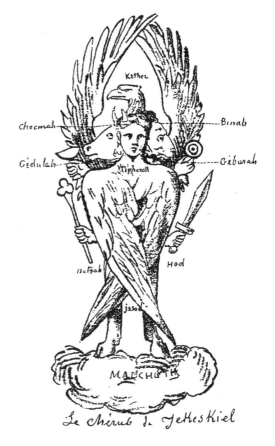

ABOVE: *Eliphas Lévi's Le Cherub de L'Ekeskiel (Cherubin of Ezekiel), from his work* Dogme et Rituel de la Haute Magie (Transcendental Magic), *1854.*

The story continues with the prominent occultist Alphonse Louis Constant, who went by his chosen name of Eliphas Lévi. In the mid-1800s, this French Rosicrucian developed the possible link between the major arcana and kabbala by explaining how the twenty-two letters of the Hebrew alphabet corresponded to the twenty-two major arcana cards of the Tarot. Lévi's illustration, *Le Cherub de L'Ekeskiel* (see top right), shows how he combined kabbala with the Tarot. He drew a cherub based on the vision of the prophet Ezekiel, as described in the Old Testament's Book of Ezekiel—this is a traditional cherub, rather than the familiar *pucci*, or chubby winged infant, that we generally envisage. Lévi's sketch shows the four holy living creatures of Ezekiel's vision: the cherub itself, the eagle, lion, and bull. But he added four hands, each of which holds an emblem of the four suits of the minor arcana: the sword, wand, pentacle, and cup. He also annotated his work with the names of the ten sephira (energy centers) of the kabbala: kether, chokmah, binah, chesed, geburah, tipereth, netzach, hod, yesod, and malkuth (see page 25). Many Tarot decks, such as the Rider Waite Smith, show card XXI, the World, with the four living creatures surrounding the garlanded dancer.

MYSTICAL ORDERS

The Hermetic Order of the Golden Dawn, a British occult society, created a system of magic that wove together the kabbalistic, astrological, and Egyptian Tarot associations. It was founded in 1888, during the occult revival, by William Wynn Westcott and William Robert Woodman, both doctors, and Samuel Liddell Mathers (later MacGregor Mathers). All three were masons. The "order" of the Golden Dawn was based on a hierarchy of ten degrees, from the ten sephira of kabbala (see page 25). It devised a list of Tarot associations that is nowadays the one most generally accepted; it presented the element, the planetary influence,

ABOVE: *The Chariot*, Oswald Wirth Tarot. *The Egyptian and kabbalistic influence is evident in the Wirth Tarot. The chariot is pulled by two sphinxes, and the chariot itself is adorned by the winged sun disc of Egypt. The Hebrew letter vav appears on the lower right corner of the card.*

Tree of Life pathway, and Hebrew letter for each major arcana card.

The order also developed the divinatory meanings of the minor arcana cards, and presented fully illustrated numbered (or "pip") cards, rather than showing a simple geometric design. One leading light of the order was Arthur Edward Waite, the originator of the Rider Waite Smith Tarot deck. Waite's deck, illustrated by Pamela Colman Smith, was published in 1909 before the eventual demise of the order in 1914. The Rider Waite Smith deck is based on the card meanings of the Order of the Golden Dawn, and is still one of the most popular decks in use today.

The infamous magician Aleister Crowley was initiated into the order in 1889, yet his Tarot cards—known as the Book of Thoth, or Thoth deck—did not appear until

1944, three years before his death. The limited-edition cards were illustrated by Lady Frieda Harris and only became available to the general public much later, in 1969. Crowley, "an unspeakable mad person" according to fellow initiate W. B. Yeats, left the order in 1900 after a disagreement with MacGregor Mathers. By 1907, however, he had founded the Argentinum Astrum, or Order of the Silver Star. This was his own magical society, whose key text, *The Book of the Law*, had been channeled by Crowley himself, posing as the Prince Chioa Khan at the Great Pyramid of Egypt. Crowley's cult combined his interest in sexual magic with some of the rituals taken from the Golden Dawn.

THE LOVERS.

ABOVE: *The Lovers from the* Rider Waite Smith Tarot, *illustrated by Pamela Colman Smith and directed by A. E. Waite. The artist's insignia appears on the lower right side of the card, by the leg of the male lover.*

ABOVE: *Judgement, by American artist Beth Moon, 2002. Moon's work is inspired by the mythical and spiritual aspects of Tarot as a path of spiritual ascension.*

The Golden Dawn tradition continues today. The American occultist Paul Foster Case, who was born in 1884, was so influenced by the order and by Waite's landmark deck that he founded his own order, Builders of the Adytum (BOTA). BOTA is an international Tarot organization based in Los Angeles. It has its own black-and-white Tarot cards, illustrated by Jesse Burns Parke, which are based on the Rider Waite Smith designs. Tarot students color in the cards, following a precise code.

2 TAROT SYMBOLISM
USING ASTROLOGY
WITH THE TAROT

THE ASTROLOGICAL ASSOCIATIONS generally used in Tarot are those devised by the Hermetic Order of the Golden Dawn (see page 18). However, their original pairings of cards with the planets, zodiacal signs, and elements were based on the seven known planets that could be seen from the Earth: the Sun, Moon, Mercury, Venus, Mars, Jupiter, and Saturn. The distant planet Uranus had been discovered in 1781 (the first planet to be identified using a telescope), followed by Neptune in 1846; Pluto was not identified until 1930, after the order had officially ended. Opposite is a rectified list that includes all ten planets, plus the twelve astrological signs. It is possible to use the dates of the zodiac signs to give timings in your readings (see page 22).

LEFT: *The Ace of Coins from the* Minchiate Florentine, *a sixteenth-century Italian deck (see also the caption opposite). The card shown here is a reproduction of the original deck of 1725, which consists of ninety-seven cards. The additional cards are: the three theological virtues, Faith, Hope, and Charity; one cardinal virtue, Prudence; the four elements; and the twelve ʒodiac signs. The Pope is not included in this minchiate deck.*

PLANETARY AND ELEMENTAL ASSOCIATIONS OF THE MAJOR ARCANA

0 THE FOOL	AIR, URANUS
I THE MAGICIAN	AIR, MERCURY
II THE HIGH PRIESTESS	WATER, THE MOON
III THE EMPRESS	EARTH, VENUS
IV THE EMPEROR	FIRE, ARIES
V THE HIEROPHANT	EARTH, TAURUS
VI THE LOVERS	AIR, GEMINI
VII THE CHARIOT	WATER, CANCER
VIII JUSTICE	AIR, LIBRA
IX THE HERMIT	EARTH, VIRGO
X THE WHEEL OF FORTUNE	FIRE, JUPITER
XI STRENGTH	FIRE, LEO
XII THE HANGED MAN	WATER, NEPTUNE
XIII DEATH	WATER, SCORPIO
XIV TEMPERANCE	FIRE, SAGITTARIUS
XV THE DEVIL	EARTH, CAPRICORN
XVI THE TOWER	FIRE, MARS
XVII THE STAR	AIR, AQUARIUS
XVIII THE MOON	WATER, PISCES
XIX THE SUN	FIRE, THE SUN
XX JUDGEMENT	FIRE, PLUTO
XXI THE WORLD	EARTH, SATURN

ABOVE: *The Emperor from the* Minchiate Florentine, *1725. This deck incorporates the traditional virtues and allegories of the era with the signs of the zodiac. In some Tarots the Emperor is associated with Aries (see right); in others, with Jupiter.*

THE ELEMENTS AND THE MINOR ARCANA

The four elements are mirrors of nature itself and of the nature of human beings. Earth, Fire, Water, and Air are vital for life, and they are designed to support each other to maintain equilibrium: without Air, Fire will die; without Water, Earth cannot survive.

The four suits of the minor arcana are associated with the four elements of Earth, Fire, Water, and Air. The system of elements and their relationship to distinct energies, or personality types, dates to the fourth century BCE and Aristotle's theory on the ratio of opposites. Fire was associated with warmth, Earth was dry, Air cool, and Water moist. Even from these basic descriptions, we can see implicit character traits: cool-headed, intelligent Air signs reveal the nature of the logical Swords; receptive Water signs link with emotional Cups. This thinking can also be seen in twentieth-century psychology. Carl Jung saw the "four basic functions" of our nature as thinking, sensation, intuition, and feeling. Relating this to the elements and minor arcana suits, we get Swords/Air

as "thinking," Pentacles/Earth as "sensation," Wands/Fire as "intuition," and Cups/Water as "feeling." A simple interpretation of this theory, shown below, can act as an *aide-memoire* in a reading:

SWORDS/AIR: *I THINK*   WANDS/FIRE: *I WANT*
PENTACLES/EARTH: *I HAVE*   CUPS/WATER: *I FEEL.*

In astrology, each element relates to the three signs of the zodiac. For example, Water is the ruling element of Cancer, Scorpio, and Pisces. This system can be helpful when trying to identify a Court card, for example. The Queen of Cups will therefore be a woman born under Cancer, Scorpio, or Pisces.

CUPS: WATER
The signs of Cancer, Scorpio, and Pisces

WANDS: FIRE
The signs of Aries, Leo, and Sagittarius

PENTACLES: EARTH
The signs of Virgo, Taurus, and Capricorn

SWORDS: AIR
The signs of Gemini, Libra, and Aquarius

USING ASTROLOGY TO TIME YOUR READINGS
The four elements traditionally relate to the four seasons—Air (Sword) cards are winter; Water (Cups) cards are summer; Fire (Wands) cards are spring; and Earth (Pentacles) cards relate to fall. With the major arcana (as shown in the charts on pages 21 and 23), some of the major trumps relate to specific zodiac signs. You can use the dates for each star sign as a way to time a reading. For example, the Hermit relates to Virgo, so the influence of this card may occur between August 24 and September 23. The influence of the Devil is linked to the time of Capricorn, the goat. The Devil takes a goat-like form in many traditional decks, symbolizing his identity as Satan, Baphomet, and particularly Pan, who was half-god, half-man.

On page 23 is a list of the major arcana cards that relate to signs of the zodiac and their respective dates. For specific spreads that you can use to time your readings, see pages 53–60.

THE EMPEROR	ARIES	MARCH 21–APRIL 20
THE HIEROPHANT	TAURUS	APRIL 21–MAY 21
THE LOVERS	GEMINI	MAY 22–JUNE 21
THE CHARIOT	CANCER	JUNE 22–JULY 23
STRENGTH	LEO	JULY 24–AUGUST 23
THE HERMIT	VIRGO	AUGUST 24–SEPTEMBER 23
JUSTICE	LIBRA	SEPTEMBER 24–OCTOBER 23
DEATH	SCORPIO	OCTOBER 24–NOVEMBER 22
TEMPERANCE	SAGITTARIUS	NOVEMBER 23–DECEMBER 21
THE DEVIL	CAPRICORN	DECEMBER 22–JANUARY 20
THE STAR	AQUARIUS	JANUARY 21–FEBRUARY 19
THE MOON	PISCES	FEBRUARY 20–MARCH 20

ABOVE: *The Sun, the Moon, and the Star, from the Visconti-Sforza deck. These three cards are the cosmic cards of the Tarot. A lone female figure or a cherub hold aloft the symbol for their card, perhaps collectively signifying the potential of human spirituality.*

THE TAROT AND KABBALA

ABOVE: *The Fool*, Etteilla Spanish Tarot, *late nineteenth century. This deck includes the upright and reversed card meanings with their Hebrew letters. The letter hei appears on the Fool, so the artist did not conform to the systems of Papus, Eliphas Lévi, or MacGregor Mathers (see page 26), who linked the Fool with the letter aleph.*

KABBALA IS THE MYSTICAL BELIEF SYSTEM derived from Judaism. Many Tarot readers use the correspondences between kabbala's Tree of Life, its central symbol, and the Tarot to divine deeper meanings from the cards.

The emergence of kabbala can be linked to the *Sefer Yetzirah*, or Book of Creation. There is no exact date for its origin or distribution, but it is thought that it was written between the third and sixth centuries CE. It includes meditations that were based on the twenty-two letters of the Hebrew alphabet.

The late 1400s saw the publication of a kabbalistic classic: the *Zohar*, or Book of Splendor. Its author was believed to be the second-century rabbi Shimon ben Yohai, although Spanish kabbalist Moses De Leon, who claimed to have discovered the book, was also rumored to have written it. The *Zohar* is a commentary on the Torah, written in Aramaic. It had a significant impact on the development of kabbala as a mystical system.

The *Zohar* revealed the Tree of Life, which showed twenty-two pathways connecting the ten sephira (vortexes of energy) through which God created the world. The purpose of the tree is to show the nature of the relationships between people and the universe by means of connective pathways. The tree can also be seen as three pillars: the left side is associated with femininity and judgement; the right side with masculinity and mercy; the sephira in the central column are concerned with equilibrium, for here all the qualities of the left and right sephira must be synthesized to create wholeness and integral wisdom.

Kabbalists linked each major arcana card with one of the twenty-two pathways on the tree. By understanding the energies of the pathway and their connecting sephira, we can understand the deeper qualities of the card. The Devil, for example, links the two sephira of tipereth (meaning beauty) and hod (majesty, or glory). This may be the temptation expressed by the card when one is caught between wanting to feel powerful and choosing a path of peace.

Different sources assign slightly different meanings to the sephira, but the most widely used interpretations are given in the list below.

ABOVE: *The Tower,* Etteilla Spanish Tarot, *late nineteenth century. Etteilla, a French occultist and Tarot-card reader (see page 16), influenced the esoteric development of the Tarot.* BELOW: *The Hebrew letters tzaddi (right); pei (center); beit (left).*

KEY TO THE SEPHIRA (See illustration overleaf)

1 KETHER: CROWN, UNITY, PERFECTION

2 CHOKMAH: WISDOM

3 BINAH: UNDERSTANDING

4 CHESED: LOVE

5 GEBURAH: POWER, JUDGEMENT

6 TIPERETH: HARMONY, BEAUTY

7 NETZACH: DESIRE, STRENGTH, INSTINCT

8 HOD: MAJESTY AND THE MIND

9 YESOD: FOUNDATION, UNCONSCIOUS

10 MALKUTH: KINGDOM, EXPERIENCE

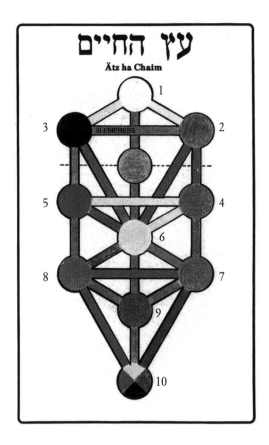

עץ החיים

Ätz ha Chaim

LEFT: *The Tree of Life Tarot, 1983, is designed to be a spiritual mirror. Each major arcana card shows the Tree of Life with its associated sephirot. See the previous page for the key to the sephira.*

KABBALA AND THE MAJOR ARCANA

There are three versions of the correspondences between the Tarot trumps and the Hebrew alphabet: those of Eliphas Lévi (see page 17), the Spanish-born occultist Papus (Dr. Gerald Encausse), and MacGregor Mathers, a key member of the Order of the Golden Dawn (see page 18). The chart below is organized according to Mathers' system, which begins with card 0, the Fool.

MAJOR ARCANA CORRESPONDENCES WITH THE HEBREW ALPHABET

CARD	HEBREW LETTER	INTERPRETATION
0 THE FOOL	ALEPH	INSTINCT
I THE MAGICIAN	BEIT	CREATIVITY
II THE HIGH PRIESTESS	GIMEL	WISDOM
III THE EMPRESS	DALED	ATTAINMENT
IV THE EMPEROR	HEI	ADVANCEMENT
V THE HIEROPHANT	VAV	KINDNESS
VI THE LOVERS	ZAYIN	SOULFULNESS
VII THE CHARIOT	CHET	GUIDANCE
VIII *STRENGTH	TET	COURAGE
IX THE HERMIT	YOD	PRUDENCE
X THE WHEEL OF FORTUNE	KAPH	DESTINY
XI *JUSTICE	LAMED	FAIRNESS

XII The Hanged Man	Mem	Transition
XIII Death	Nun	Decline; rebirth
XIV Temperance	Samekh	Patience
XV Devil	Ayin	Clear vision
XVI The Tower	Pei	Chaos
XVII The Star	Tzaddi	Hope
XVIII The Moon	Kaph	Hidden problems
XIX The Sun	Resh	Success
XX Judgement	Shin	Renewal
XXI The World	Tav	Completion

* Note that the position of Strength and Justice is reversed in the Golden Dawn system.

Kabbala and The Minor Arcana

Eliphas Lévi established a link between the four suits of the minor arcana and the Tetragrammaton, or four Hebrew letters, that represent the Yahweh or Jehovah, the name of God: YHVH (Y = suit of Wands, H = Cups, V = Swords, H = Pentacles). The numbered minor arcana cards are linked with their associated numbered sephira, as shown below.

Sephirot Number and Minor Arcana Card

1 Kether: Unity, perfection	Aces
2 Chokmah: Wisdom	Twos
3 Binah: Understanding	Threes
4 Chesed: Love	Fours
5 Geburah: Power, judgement	Fives
6 Tipereth: Harmony, beauty	Sixes
7 Netzach: Desire, strength, instinct	Sevens
8 Hod: Majesty and the mind	Eights
9 Yesod: Foundation, unconscious	Nines
10 Malkuth: Kingdom, experience	Tens

ABOVE: *The Aleph, or Fool, card from a modern Tarot kabbala deck. The letter aleph appears at the lower corners.*
LEFT: *Hebrew letters tet (right); kaph (left).*

THE TAROT MENAGERIE

The Tarot speaks in the language of symbols,
the language of the unconscious, and when approached
in the right manner it may open a door into the hidden
reaches of the soul.

ALFRED DOUGLAS, *The Tarot*

IN THE CARDS OF THE MAJOR ARCANA, animals appear as symbols of our deepest instincts. They act as messengers or reminders of our mortality, of the fluctuating cycles of birth, death, and rebirth over which we have little control. The animals of the Tarot range from the domestic dog of the Fool to the mythic dragon of the Wheel of Fortune, and from the snake of the Hermit to the wolves of the Moon. Understanding their significance in the Tarot can be allied to interpreting animals in our dreams, because they too help us access important information from the unconscious.

THE SNAKE: INSTINCT

The snake appears on card IX, entwined around the staff of the Hermit. As earth-dwellers, snakes are perceived in many cultures as symbols of fertility. In Greek mythology, serpents or dragons were said to pull the chariot of the earth goddess Demeter. In Hindu myth, however, snakes appear as evil *nagas,* and in Christianity as an agent of corruption in the Garden of Eden. Yet the Hermit's snake is not out of control: the tamed snake symbolizes his instinctive wisdom and a fertile mind that will guide him through the underworld of the unconscious.

THE CRAYFISH: THE SOUL

On card XVIII, the Moon, a crayfish or lobster is part submerged in water, while its upper body makes a primitive cry toward the light of the moon. In mythology, fish represent the soul, our deepest level of instinct. In the Fenian cycle of Irish legends, the warrior hero, Finn, eats a magical salmon that gives him knowledge of all things. Early Christians used the fish as a secret sign of their faith, which links to the meaning of the card as a whole: a crisis of faith.

THE HORSE: CONFLICT AND PASSION

Horses appear throughout the minor arcana on all the Knight cards. This indicates that they are essentially the action men of the Court cards, speeding up events and signaling change and possibly adventure. In the major arcana, horses appear on card VII, the Chariot. The charioteer is successful through the force of his personality, carefully harnessing life's conflicts and obstacles, which are symbolized by the white and dark horses. In psychological terms, the harnessed horses symbolize libido under control.

THE LION: STRENGTH

A symbol of sovereignty, the lion is often associated with supreme power, strength, and even destruction. The Egyptian lion-headed goddess, Sekhmet, was sent by the sun god to annihilate a human rebellion; in Greek mythology, Herakles's first labor was to

kill the terrifying lion of Nemea. In the Visconti-Sforza Strength card (left), a man subdues a lion with threatened force. In Rider Waite Smith Tarots, a woman holds the jaws of the lion, taming him with gentleness. The lion alongside this figure of civility, or higher self, shows the reconciliation of opposite aspects of human nature.

THE DRAGON: PRIMAL POWER

The dragon appears on many Wheel of Fortune cards, as a miniature figure of Justice brandishing a sword with which he judges the soul of humans and guards the underworld. The dragon symbolizes the primal energy of nature.

THE MONKEY: VANITY

The monkey represents vanity and impermanence. He is often shown clambering on the side of the Wheel of Fortune, or grinding the wheel itself, as the other beasts or people rise and fall at his will.

THE ASS: FOLLY

The ass or donkey is a traditional symbol of folly, but also represents submission. Christ chose this lowliest of animals to carry him into Jerusalem as a symbol of humility. On the Wheel of Fortune, the ass is often shown clinging to the wheel itself, powerless against the force of the turning world.

THE DOG: CONSCIENCE

The dog appears on the Fool card, pawing at his distracted master, like a bad attack of his conscience. As with all animals in the Tarot, the dog represents primitive urges—here, a natural desire to protect another from danger—that are inherent for our survival.

THE TAROT RAINBOW

COLORS ARE OFTEN USED IN THE TAROT AS A CODE. In decks such as the Marseilles, some Tarot scholars have deconstructed the use of color and assigned particular significance to those used. However, as with all art forms, practicality is an important factor. The four or five basic colors used on the original Marseilles deck would have reflected what was available to the printers at the time, or what was economically viable for the card makers to use. In the early hand-painted decks made for kings and dukes, expensive colors may have been more feasible.

It is important to refer to your own particular deck when interpreting colors, as some have their own color systems. Opposite is a list of common colors and associations.

RED

Creativity and vitality; the material world. The Magician traditionally wears a red robe to suggest his energy. Some Tarot decks use red as a theme for the Swords cards, due to its association with the blood of conflict.

BLACK

Endings, fear, the shadow self. The Chariot's black horse (see page 80) represents his shadow side that must be controlled, while the black baying wolves of the Moon (see page 102) can signify fear.

YELLOW

The intellect, logic, and self-expression. Some Tarot decks use yellow as a theme for the Swords, or for Pentacles, because yellow is associated with Earth, the element of the latter suit.

BLUE

Communication, intuition, and truth. The High Priestess often wears blue like Isis, the Egyptian madonna (see page 73). Some Tarots use blue as a theme for Cups, to signify its element, Water. In Temperance (left) blue also symbolizes water, for managing emotions.

GREEN

Nature, fertility, love, and protection. In the Visconti-Sforza deck (right), the Empress has green hands, to show her fertility.

Some Tarot decks use green as a theme for the suit of Wands.

NATURALS

Natural colors such as beige and cream can denote material issues and sacrifice. In the Visconti-Sforza Tarot deck, the half-clothed, impoverished Fool is a symbol of the self-sacrifice of Lent.

WHITE

White symbolizes purity, perfection, and innocence. The Rider Waite Smith Tarot card for the Sun shows a child riding a white horse, which denotes innocence.

3 How to Lay the Cards
Tarot Readings

Choosing a Deck

It is important to choose a deck that you really like. You will have it for a long time and you have to live with it; people rarely give away their cards, so unless you inherit an unwanted Tarot deck, you will need to purchase your own. There are so-called traditions that dictate that you should not buy your own cards, but that they should be bought for you as a gift. Do not worry about this—choosing cards is such a personal experience that it would be difficult to rely on someone else to do this for you.

If you have not bought a Tarot deck before, try one that has illustrated "pip" or numbered cards, such as the Rider Waite Smith deck. The images on the card will stir your memory if you already have some familiarity with the Tarot, or will help you learn the card meanings from scratch. However, decks with geometric suit designs for the numbered cards are preferred by some readers who feel limited rather than inspired by minor arcana pictorial imagery.

Always treat your Tarot cards with respect. Keep them wrapped in a dark cloth, preferably in a box or drawer. They are personal to you, so do not leave them on display for others to touch. It is important that they absorb your energy as you continually handle them. This is why some Tarotists recommend sleeping with a new deck under your pillow for the first few weeks after purchase.

Shown opposite is a list of well-known decks and their country of origin or style. This is a very small selection and is not intended to be comprehensive.

ABOVE: *The Queen of Pentacles from the* Tarot of Marseilles. *The Marseilles is one of the most influential decks in the history of Tarot (see pages 10, 13, 33).*

FRANCE
TAROT OF MARSEILLES (1761) Painted by artist Nicolas Conver, master papermaker at Marseilles (left).

GERMANY
ZIGEUNER TAROT (1975) Designed by Walter Wegmuller. Richly illustrated, these cards show Hebrew letters and the traditional Arabic numerals.

ITALY
VISCONTI-SFORZA TAROTS Reproductions of fifteenth-century Tarot decks (see pages 9, 13, 23, 64, 155).

JAPAN
UKIYOE TAROT (1982) Art-directed by Stuart R. Kaplan and painted by Koji Furuta in the style of the *ukiyo-e* art tradition, which flourished in Japan during the mid-seventeenth century.

ABOVE: *The Star from* The Crystal Tarot *illustrated by Elisabetta Trevisan.*

SWITZERLAND
IJJ SWISS TAROT A traditional late-eighteenth- to early nineteenth-century pack, in which the Pope (Hierophant) and the Papess (High Priestess) are replaced by the gods Jupiter and Juno, giving the pack its JJ moniker.

UNITED KINGDOM
RIDER WAITE SMITH TAROT (1909) Illustrated by Pamela Colman Smith, directed by A. E. Waite, a leading member of the Hermetic Order of the Golden Dawn (see page 18).

MYTHIC TAROT (1986) Written and art-directed by Juliet Sharman-Burke and Liz Greene, and illustrated by Tricia Newell. A fully illustrated Tarot based on Greek mythology.

UNITED STATES
SACRED ROSE TAROT (1982) Illustrated by Johanna Sherman and inspired by the sacred lotus of the Orient. The "pip" cards are fully illustrated.

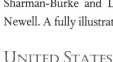

ABOVE: *The* Zigeuner Tarot *(1975) by gypsy artist Walter Wegmuller.*

WHEN TO READ THE CARDS

When reading for yourself, make it a habit to read when you feel that you don't need to. This may sound contrary to the traditional view of needing a reading because you have decisions to make, or other pressing events about which you seek clarity. However, reading the cards when you don't have an urgent question can help you develop a more detached attitude. When you interpret your own cards, it is tempting to see what you want to see. If you are a beginner, try reading for yourself alongside a friend, speaking your reading aloud.

Start by reading for yourself once a week. Keep a Tarot diary, and note the cards that come up each time. Vary the spreads that you use—start with a three-card spread and progress to more complex arrangements as you gain confidence. And pay attention to the patterns of cards, because you will find that over time certain ones recur. Get to know them well.

ABOVE: *A card showing hexagram 13, (Tung Jen) from* The I Ching of Love, *which reproduces the 64 hexagrams of the ancient Chinese oracle.*

READING REVERSED CARDS

While shuffling, some cards naturally reverse. A reversed card is upside down, and in a Tarot reading its meaning is different from that of a card in the upright position. Often, reversed cards can have more negative meanings than upright ones, but several, such as the Five of Cups, have a more positive interpretation.

You can choose to use reversals or not. Many readers do not read reversals—if they arise in a spread, they simply turn them the right way up before beginning to read. However, it's helpful to know both the upright and reversed meanings of a card, and see which one speaks to you, regardless of the card's position. The key issue is to follow your intuition, working with the cards to illuminate potential paths and choices in ways that resonate for you.

PILE 1   PILE 2   PILE 3

1 MIDDLE   2 TOP   3 BOTTOM

*Cut the deck into three piles from left to right
(see top row). If you choose pile 2, pile 2 goes on
top, with pile 1 under it, and pile 3 on the bottom.*

PREPARING FOR A READING

In Tarot, ritual can help to calm the mind. Like laying the table before eating a meal, so you should prepare a clean surface and lay down the cloth in which you wrap your cards. Some Tarot readers light a candle before they begin, because this symbolizes passing from one state to the next; the candle is extinguished when the reading is over.

Shuffle the cards as you think of a question or an event that you would like illuminated. If you do not have anything specific to ask, just be in the moment. Stop shuffling when you feel calm and ready. Shuffling the deck is an important part of the Tarot ritual because it helps you focus your attention on the present—this is the yoga of Tarot practice. Then take the shuffled deck and, with your left hand (traditionally this represents the hand of fate), cut the deck into three piles. Choose one pile, then place the other piles underneath it as shown above. Your chosen pile should be on top. If you are reading for someone else, ask them to shuffle the cards so that they imprint them with their personal energy. Then ask them to choose a pile. Take this pile from them, then gather up the remaining two piles, as explained above.

When the deck is ready, lay out your cards in a spread (see overleaf). Turn the cards face up from left to right or right to left. If you flip them top to bottom, you reverse the card's aspect, which affects its meaning (see Reading reversed cards, opposite).

THREE–CARD READINGS

Threes make a story: a beginning, middle, and end. You can start by using just three cards to create a Tarot story that describes the past, present, and future. Use this arrangement for an overview or to detail one aspect of life, such as career or relationships. Shuffle and cut the cards, then lay them out as shown.

1   2   3

SAMPLE READING: RELATIONSHIPS

CARD 1: PAST
CARD 2: PRESENT
CARD 3: FUTURE

1   2   3

The querent wanted to find out about future relationships as she had just left a long-term partner. The cards drawn are the Eight of Cups, the Nine of Cups, and the Knight of Swords.

The Eight of Cups is in the past position, which shows that there has been dissatisfaction in an established relationship, and that the querent was not getting what she needed from this partnership.

The Nine of Cups shows that she is now much happier and can have whatever she wishes for. This is a good time to meet a new partner.

Her future is the Knight of Swords in shining armor: a professional, charming individual who may bring a whirlwind romance—but also drama; events will unfold quickly. To find out more about the Knight, we chose an additional card, the Ace of Wands. This indicates beginnings and passion, so overall it is likely that the querent's potential relationship will bring excitement, along with a degree of upheaval.

SAMPLE READING: TRAVEL

1 2 3

CARD 1: PAST
CARD 2: PRESENT
CARD 3: FUTURE

The querent has been thinking of taking time off from work and traveling around Asia. He wants to know how feasible his plans are. The cards drawn are the Eight of Wands, the Ace of Pentacles, and the Chariot.

The Eight of Wands is in the past position. This shows that he has made progress in his life and has made good connections—bringing exciting opportunities. He has lots of options available to him.

The Ace of Pentacles is in the present position. He has the money or, if not just at present, will find it very soon—a time of prosperity and success beckons.

The Chariot reveals that the querent will physically travel because his determination will make it possible.

SAMPLE READING: MONEY, WORK, AND LOVE

CARD 1: MONEY
CARD 2: CAREER
CARD 3: LOVE

1 2 3

The querent did not have a pressing question, so we used three cards for insight into her three key life areas: money, work, and love. The cards drawn are the Magician, the World, and the Emperor.

Since three major arcana cards have been drawn, important change can be expected. The Magician appears as the money card. While the querent is not well off, she has all the talent she needs to make money appear out of thin air. This is a creative time for her—her horizons are expanding.

The World is her career card. She is near the end of a particular phase of work; she may even be thinking of changing her career. She has been successful so far, but the start of a new enterprise is close at hand, and she can look forward to it.

The Emperor is the querent's love card. In a woman's reading, the Emperor often denotes her husband. Here, it represents her long-term partner, who could give her stability as she undergoes major changes in her career and finances.

The Heart and Head Spread

Card 4: The heart of the
    matter
Card 1: Your spiritual self
Card 2: What you think
Card 3: What you feel

1

3

This simple spread uses the major arcana only. This reveals the spiritual, intellectual, and emotional aspects of your life, along with a card that acts as a key to the whole reading. You can read this spread predictively, but I find it a good spread for personal reflection, too.

2

4

Remove all the minor arcana cards from the deck, then shuffle and cut the remaining twenty-two cards, laying down four as shown. Read card 4 first, and interpret the other cards in the light of this.

1

2

3

4

Sample Reading: Leaving Work

The querent is taking early retirement from work and wants to look at a number of issues relating to the end of her present career. The cards drawn are the Chariot, Justice, the Hermit, and Temperance.

Card 4: The heart of the matter is Temperance. The querent is managing several situations that are potentially explosive. She is working hard, weighing up her finances until her layoff payment, and dealing with potentially precarious individuals whom she needs to rely on right now. She requires emotional balance during a stressful time.

CARD 1: The Chariot represents the querent's spirituality and her hopes for herself. This card reveals that she will make sure progress. It is likely she will travel in the future, or generally be spending more time away from home. New adventures await her, so she is looking forward to the next phase of her life.

CARD 2: Justice appears in the thinking position, which is apt given that the querent wants her decision to be justified, and wants to be fairly treated financially and have her past work acknowledged. She wants all legal agreements to be signed and sealed so that she can take up her chariot and move on.

CARD 3: The Hermit reveals how the querent feels. It shows that she feels a little alone on her path to seek the life that she wants. This can manifest as a desire for time out to recuperate after she leaves her job. The Hermit also reveals that things will take time. If we relate this card to Justice, then finalizing contracts may take a bit longer than expected.

SAMPLE READING: LOVE AND SECURITY

1

2

3

The querent has a good relationship with his partner, with whom he does not live. He would like some insight into issues of commitment for the future. The cards drawn are the Empress, the Sun, the Moon, and the Devil.

CARD 4: The heart of the matter is the Empress. This is the querent's partner. She represents home life and the desire for love, stability, and, perhaps, a family.

4

CARD 1: The Sun in this spiritual-self position reflects the querent's hopes for joy and security. The Sun card shows a sanctuary of happiness, the spiritual ideal of a relationship. The querent wants a life in the sun in an environment in which he is looked after, perhaps by his partner.

CARDS 2 AND 3: The Devil appears in the thinking position, and the Moon reveals the querent's emotions. These two cards link with one another, because they reveal subconscious doubt and an awareness of a pending decision. The Moon shows an element of disillusion that his present relationship can be lived in the sun, which makes him fear restriction, as symbolized by the Devil. If he fears commitment, he must soon decide what is best for their relationship.

THE STAR SPREAD

CARD 4: THE HEART OF THE MATTER

CARD 1: THE PRESENT

CARD 2: FEELINGS

CARD 3: THOUGHTS

CARD 5: THE SUBCONSCIOUS: WHAT
IS HIDDEN AND WILL SURFACE

CARD 6: WHAT YOU DESIRE

CARD 7: THE OUTCOME

7

6

5

4

3

2

The Star is a popular spread with Tarot readers, and it can be particularly insightful when you use only the major arcana cards; this gives spreads such as this, which use fewer cards, a dedicated focus. Shuffle, cut, and lay out the cards as shown above. Interpret card 4, the heart of the matter, before the other cards, as this anchors your reading.

1

SAMPLE READING: WILL THE PAST BE PUT TO REST?

The querent has been looking back at past issues that have been troubling her for some time. She wants to know if she can resolve and heal the past.

CARD 4: The querent's card is the Tower. It shows that her beliefs or way of living are being undermined. She is experiencing a testing and even fearful time; she may feel that she has little that is concrete to hold on to. However, this sudden collapse will be liberating in the long term, after the shock subsides.

CARD 1: This shows where the querent is at present, and here the Death card makes an appearance. She is dealing with an important ending in one area of her life, and it is time to let go of the past. Along with the Tower, Death is confirmation that major changes are under way.

CARD 2: The card in this position represents the querent's feelings about her situation, here symbolized by the World. She knows deep down that she is ready to move on, and that by rights she needs a fresh start.

CARD 3: The Hermit reflects how the querent has intellectualized her situation. The card shows that she has analyzed past issues in her own way, and is on a personal quest to find answers. The card also suggests she needs to follow her own path.

CARDS 5 AND 6: Card 5, the Devil, is the querent's subconscious at work. She will need to make a mature decision if she is to make progress; she may be tempted to stay where she is, perhaps repeating old patterns of behavior. This decision is important if she is to achieve the ambition of card 6, the Star, which reveals her known desires. She would love to feel inspired and hopeful, and revitalized rather than drained.

CARD 7: The Magician is a great card here, because it shows that the outcome will be positive. The Magician is a wonderful symbol of energy, creativity, and in some cases travel; he deals with the present and looks to the future. Unlike the Hermit, the Magician shows off his talent to others, so it appears as if the querent finds a way to express herself, rather than be overly reflective. She will move on and opportunities will beckon. Getting to this stage, however, feels like a long process just now, but with patience and self-belief, she can look forward to her future with optimism.

THE PAST, PRESENT, AND FUTURE SPREAD

CARD 1: YOUR PRESENT CIRCUMSTANCES

CARD 2: THE PAST

CARD 3: PAST CHALLENGES

CARD 4: LESSONS AND GUIDANCE

CARD 5: NEW INFLUENCES ABOUT TO ENTER YOUR LIFE

CARD 6: HOW THEY WILL AFFECT YOU

CARD 7: THE OUTCOME

This seven-card spread is a good preliminary to the Celtic Cross (see page 45). The pattern of the spread consists of two three-card sequences for the past and future, with a single card for the present. Shuffle and cut the cards, dealing seven cards face down from the top of the deck as shown.

VARIATION

To get more information about a card you have already laid down, select four more cards from the top of the deck and lay them around your chosen card as shown overleaf. Read them in turn as described, as their meanings will provide four additional aspects of the situation.

SAMPLE READING: CAREER OVERVIEW

The querent did not have a specific question, but wanted a general overview of past, present, and future influences surrounding her career.

CARD 1: The querent's present circumstances are represented by the Chariot: through determined effort, she is forging ahead in her career. We laid four more cards around this one (see Variation, overleaf).

CARD 2: The past is represented by the Three of Wands. This shows that the querent's past work has been recognized by others. It is likely that she works in a creative field, or has had a good opportunity to express her ideas in her career.

CARDS 3 AND 4: The Hermit reveals past challenges—what she felt and believed about her situation. She felt that she took an intellectual approach to her work, but this set her apart from others, since she had to look within herself to find answers; she may have worked alone at home. What she learned is summarized by the Two of Pentacles, for positive choices and solvency. This also indicates a good business partnership, which may have sparked new ideas.

CARD 5: The Seven of Swords reveals new influences that are about to enter the querent's life. The Seven shows conflict and the need to use her intellect to negotiate some challenging situations.

CARD 6: The Eight of Wands illuminates the impact that these new events and feelings will have. It shows that the hard work of the Seven of Swords pays off, and she will be rewarded with lots of opportunities to shine, and possibly to travel.

CARD 7: The Seven of Pentacles is the outcome. The querent will need to stay focused and work hard for promotion. As the Three of Wands in the past has shown, there have been, and are, rewards along the way, but lots of effort will be needed at each stage. The message here is to persevere.

THE FOUR ASPECTS OF THE PRESENT

1: PRESENT CIRCUMSTANCES

1a: HIGHEST POTENTIAL

1b: WORK AND PROJECTS

1c: MONEY

1d: MOVEMENT

1a

1d   1   1b

1c

1a

1d   1   1b

VARIATION

Four additional cards were chosen to surround Card 1, the Chariot, because the querent wanted more insight into her present situation. The cards chosen were the Sun, the Star, the Knight of Cups, and the Knight of Wands. It is likely that the querent will see some rapid changes very soon, since the two Knights indicate the speeding up of events. She may have a job or new

1c

project that will further her ambitions. The Knight of Wands can also represent relocation, so she may move to a new job, or need to travel at short notice. This will provide satisfaction along with reward and inspiration, symbolized by the Sun and the Star. Under the Chariot is the Knight of Cups, an individual who may not be able to keep his promises. If this is a new boss, he may not give her adequate support with the difficulties that await with the Seven of Swords, card 5 in the main reading.

The Celtic Cross

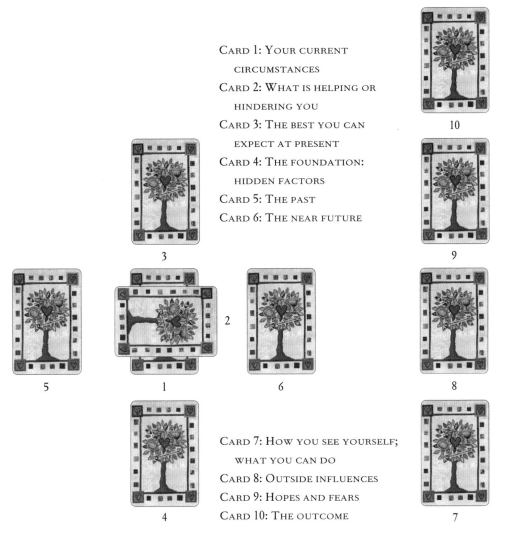

Card 1: Your current circumstances

Card 2: What is helping or hindering you

Card 3: The best you can expect at present

Card 4: The foundation: hidden factors

Card 5: The past

Card 6: The near future

Card 7: How you see yourself; what you can do

Card 8: Outside influences

Card 9: Hopes and fears

Card 10: The outcome

The Celtic Cross is a traditional and popular spread that explores general life influences and events, and illuminates the different energies at play. This layout can vary: some readers place Card 3 to the right of the cross and continue clockwise. Choose whichever method feels right for you.

Shuffle and cut the deck as usual, then deal ten cards from the top as shown.

SAMPLE READING: HOW WILL MY WORK BE RECEIVED?

The querent is a painter who is nearing the end of a difficult commission. He wants to know if his work will be well received, and if more commissions will result. He needs to rest, but knows he must look for new work if he is going to survive financially.

10

9

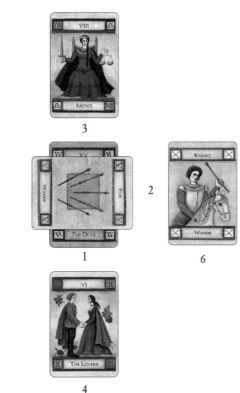

5   1   6

3

2

8

4

7

CARDS 1 AND 2: The Devil is crossed by the Five of Wands. The Devil shows that the querent feels tied to an unsatisfactory situation that is causing worry and conflict. The Five of Wands reveals that he is under pressure, and faces a situation that he has not previously encountered—which is why he does not know which way to turn. Together, these cards show that he has felt restricted and unrewarded in his work. The challenges of this commission are new to him—he may be dealing with a difficult and demanding client. There may also be a problem with a contract here, suggested by the Devil; if so, it is important that he takes action now, and begins by re-checking every detail of any important paperwork.

CARD 3: Justice is the best that the querent can hope for at this time—he will be fairly treated in a testing situation, and any contractual issues should be finalized to his satisfaction. He will feel that any action taken by him regarding his client will be justified: it is therefore likely that his work will be accepted, but he will make a resolution not to dwell on past difficulties of the work, and look ahead.

CARDS 4 AND 5: The Lovers and the Seven of Swords look at any hidden elements that may be contributing to the present situation and past circumstances. The Lovers card shows that the querent has made a commitment to himself and his work, and may have taken a risk to do so. The Swords card can indicate a lack of trust prior to the work beginning, which has now magnified in the form of the central card, the Devil.

CARD 6: The querent's next move is represented by the Knight of Wands. This reveals that events will speed up, and new offers of work should arrive. The Wands are cards of creativity, so this indicates that he has no need to worry about being out of employment for too long.

CARD 7: The Star reveals how the querent will see himself at this time. He will find his muse again as he puts the present situation behind him. He can recover his creativity and inspiration.

CARD 8: The card in position 8 shows attitudes around the querent, and the general influences impacting upon him. He will feel at one with the world, and feel happier and more secure financially, symbolized by the Sun. He may also take a well-earned vacation to sunnier climes. Other people will respond positively to him, perhaps offering him the sanctuary of their home for a short holiday.

CARD 9: The Four of Wands reveals the querent's hopes and fears. This card shows that he can hope for appreciation and establishment.

CARD 10: The outcome to the querent's present situation is represented by the Four of Swords. This shows a time for healing and recuperation after struggle—so the querent will be able to rest after an intense period of work. In this sense, the Four of Swords is a continuation of the idea of card 8, the Sun: a tranquil haven.

We can also look at the combined meaning of the two Fours here, cards 9 and 10. Two fours together traditionally indicate that there will be a good time of stability ahead.

THE TREE OF LIFE SPREAD

CARD 1: KETHER: SPIRITUALITY

CARD 2: CHOKMAH: WHAT IS TO BE
REALIZED

CARD 3: BINAH: WHAT YOU
UNDERSTAND

CARD 4: CHESED: WHAT SUPPORTS
YOU

CARD 5: GEBURAH: TESTS

CARD 6: TIPERETH: THE ISSUE OR
PROBLEM

CARD 7: NETZACH: DESIRE

CARD 8: HOD: CONSCIOUS THOUGHTS

CARD 9: YESOD: THE UNCONSCIOUS

CARD 10: MALKUTH: OUTCOME;
WHAT MATERIALIZES

VARIATION—OPTIONAL
SIGNIFICATOR CARD: DAATH:
WELL-BEING AND BALANCE

1

3

2

(S), OPTIONAL

4

5

6

7

8

9

10

This meditative spread is helpful when you have a lot going on in your life. Like the Celtic Cross, it assists you in separating life themes and events into specific areas. This spread is based on the Tree of Life, the core symbol of kabbala (see page 24). Each card represents a sephirot, or energy center, on the Tree, which has various interpretations, just some of which are given here.

Shuffle and split the deck as previously described (see page 35), then lay out ten cards in the sequence shown.

VARIATION

You can also add a significator card to the spread. Deal this card last and place it directly under card 1, kether. This represents the sephirot daath. Daath relates to your well-being and spiritual development—this is how you balance heaven and earth.

SAMPLE READING: RELOCATION

The querent has two homes. She is hoping to sell her city apartment to move to her home in the countryside. She wanted some clarity on her situation and to see if the move would work out for her. For this reading, the querent chose not to select a significator card.

CARD 1: SPIRITUAL INFLUENCES

The Seven of Cups shows that the querent sees many possibilities, but she needs a clearer vision of how living away from the city might materialize. Her imagination is consequently in overdrive.

CARD 2: WHAT IS TO BE REALIZED

This card position also shows the querent's relationship with the men in her life. The Six of Cups reveals reunions with old friends and those people from her past who, in helping with her new home, are helping her create her future. The querent is taking the good things from her past experiences and making them work for her.

CARD 3: WHAT YOU UNDERSTAND

This card position also shows she appreciates her relationships with women in her life. The Three of Cups reveals that she will soon be celebrating some good news and meeting supportive female friends.

1

2

3

4

5

6

8

7

9

10

CARD 4: WHAT SUPPORTS YOU

Temperance shows that the querent needs to look after the detail just now—she must tend the balance of her life, managing two homes in two locations until her city apartment is sold. She will soon be dealing with contracts and other legal affairs. She will manage this.

CARD 5: TESTS

The Seven of Wands shows that the querent hopes that all her hard work will pay off. She may meet some competition along the way or experience a minor delay to her plans, so she will need energy during this period, and to put her interests first.

CARD 6: THE ISSUE OR PROBLEM

The position of card 6 also reveals what is in the querent's heart. Here, she has the Ace of Swords reversed, showing a time of frustration and delay before she can relax and enjoy her country home. However, the card in this position may simply outline her fears about being held up, because the surrounding cards are very positive.

CARD 7: DESIRE

The Eight of Swords shows restriction on the romantic front, which is not surprising given that all the querent's energy is being dedicated to work and home at this time. An additional layer of meaning is feeling powerless while she is waiting for her apartment to sell.

CARD 8: CONSCIOUS THOUGHTS

The Three of Pentacles can show tradespeople. The meaning of this card here may be the building of a little empire. The querent will soon be dealing with builders through whom her ideas can take shape.

CARD 9: THE UNCONSCIOUS

The Tower is the querent's card of the unconscious or hidden issues. On a practical level, she is leaving a safe fortress for the unknown and feels vulnerable. The insecurity she may be feeling now is perhaps the aftershock that follows a life-changing decision. The card can also represent a fear that everything will fall apart.

CARD 10: OUTCOME; WHAT MATERIALIZES

The Page of Cups brings invitations, conversations, and ideas. The Tower collapses, but the world still turns. The querent will soon receive good news.

THE HORSESHOE SPREAD

1

2

7

6

CARD 1: THE PAST
CARD 2: THE PRESENT
CARD 3: FUTURE CONDITIONS
CARD 4: THE BEST PATH TO
   FOLLOW
CARD 5: ATTITUDES AROUND YOU
CARD 6: OBSTACLES
CARD 7: THE OUTCOME

3

4

5

This is a classic spread to call on when you need an answer to a specific question. The Horseshoe can have either five or seven cards; a seven-card reading is shown here. Shuffle and cut the cards as usual, then lay them out as shown.

SAMPLE READING: WILL MY FINANCES IMPROVE?

The querent has had to take out loans to finance his debts. He is self-employed and needs to pay tax in the coming months, and is doubtful if he can keep up his repayments. The cards chosen are the Ace of Pentacles, the Seven of Wands, the Ace of Swords, the Three of Pentacles, the Empress, the Ten of Wands, and the Moon.

CARD 1: The Ace of Pentacles shows that the querent has been successful with money in the past. He may have had a windfall or other cash gift.

CARD 2: The present shows the Seven of Wands: he is fighting off demands on his time and money, and will need to work hard to get the security that he hopes for.

CARD 3: The Ace of Swords reveals that he will succeed, provided he has a strategy.

CARD 4: The Three of Pentacles shows attention to detail, hard work, and creativity. If he presents ideas to clients, he will be rewarded with new work.

CARD 5: The Empress reveals that others will be generous and understanding. The downside of this card is that people may assume that the querent is not struggling, since they are used to him being financially capable.

CARD 6: The Ten of Wands predicts that the querent may be overburdened with responsibility. This may also reflect his attitude: things may get on top of him and he may feel paralyzed by indecision, rather than driven to act to resolve his debts.

CARD 7: The outcome is the Moon, which reveals a crisis of faith and indecision, as indicated by the previous card. The querent therefore needs to act now to improve his situation, rather than wait until the repayments become a serious burden. The Ace of Swords shows that he can extricate himself from his debt and win.

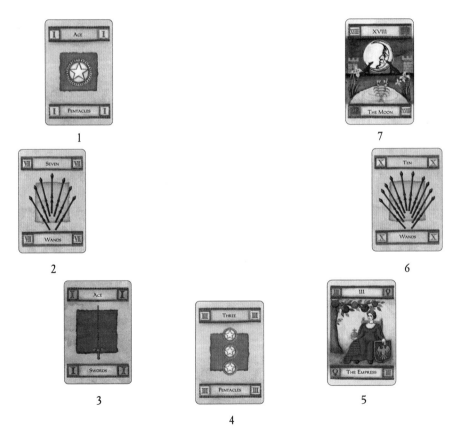

The Year Ahead Spread

Cards 1–12: Card 1 represents the first
month from the date of the reading

Card 2: This shows the events of
the next month, and so on for
twelve months

Card 13: This reveals the tone of the
year ahead

In the Year Ahead Spread, one card is laid out for each month of the year, plus a central card 13. After shuffling and cutting the deck as usual, the first card from the top of the deck is placed in the nine o'clock position, followed by the others in a counterclockwise direction as shown.

SAMPLE READING: WHAT THE NEXT YEAR HOLDS

The querent wanted a sense of what the next twelve months had in store, in terms of her work and social life.

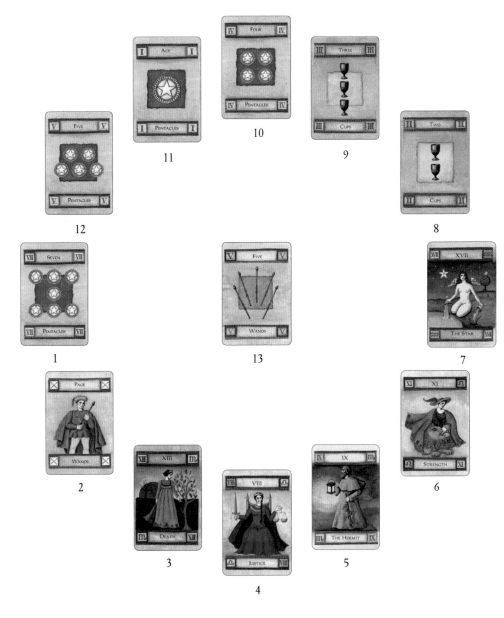

CARD 13: The theme of the year ahead is revealed by the Five of Wands. This shows the need for the querent to stand firm and stay true to her principles, regardless of external pressures. It reveals an eventful but testing twelve months ahead.

CARD 1: Month one has the Seven of Pentacles, which represents ongoing work and the potential for success. In her career and new home, the querent needs to persevere.

CARD 2: In month two, the Page of Wands brings some welcome fun and fresh inspiration. The querent will soon hear about an opportunity, but she needs to be practical too, and resist the temptation to take on too much too soon.

CARDS 3, 4, 5, AND 6: The next four months reveal a run of major arcana cards initiated by Death, which shows an ending and a new beginning. The querent will undergo some major changes during this time as she leaves behind one way of living. Justice shows that she is rewarded morally and will be dealt with fairly; legal issues will be resolved to her liking. The Hermit heralds a time to recuperate, and an element of delay. She will be eager to move forward but is held back, although this provides an opportunity to process recent events and learn from her experiences. The Strength card shows that she will need to be patient, and even emotionally strong in order to support others.

CARD 7: Month seven sees the end of a testing time. Inspiration, energy, and success arrive as the querent begins to feel at one with the rest of the world. The Star brings creative opportunities and vitality. Her dream will come true.

CARD 8: Month eight brings the Two of Cups and an intimate partnership, born from the happy environment of the previous card, the Star. If this is not a romantic alliance, then the querent will meet a new friend who becomes a soulmate.

CARD 9: Month nine is a time to look forward to, as friendship, celebrations, and light-heartedness prevail with the Three of Cups.

CARD 10: Month ten reveals the Four of Pentacles, showing security, satisfaction, and deserved rewards for work.

CARD 11: Month eleven brings the Ace of Pentacles; this will be a great time for career and money, so a pay rise may be given or an unexpected check arrive.

CARD 12: Month twelve shows a reversal of the good fortune of the Ace, but this may relate to feeling abandoned socially, rather than suffering financial lack. Help and support will be available.

THE MONTH AHEAD SPREAD

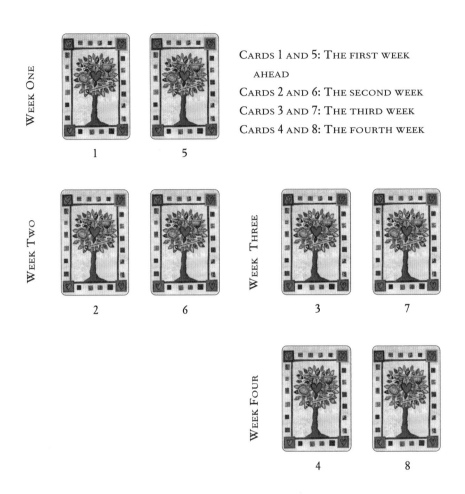

CARDS 1 AND 5: THE FIRST WEEK
  AHEAD
CARDS 2 AND 6: THE SECOND WEEK
CARDS 3 AND 7: THE THIRD WEEK
CARDS 4 AND 8: THE FOURTH WEEK

WEEK ONE

1   5

WEEK TWO

2   6

WEEK THREE

3   7

WEEK FOUR

4   8

Laying two cards for each week gives you two aspects for a broader interpretation. Shuffle and cut the deck as usual, following the layout shown.

SAMPLE READING: WORK FOR THE NEXT FOUR WEEKS

The querent wanted to know how her work would progress over the next month. She had submitted some ideas to her manager, and was hoping that she would soon have some positive feedback.

WEEK ONE: The cards drawn are the Six of Cups and the Ace of Pentacles. This will be a profitable and possibly innovative week workwise, symbolized by the Ace; the querent will be feeling balanced and settled, signified by the Six.

WEEK TWO: The Nine of Cups and the Star show that it is likely that she will be recognized for her ideas. The Nine is also the "wish" card, so whatever she wishes for now can become a reality.

WEEK THREE: The Eight of Swords and Temperance reveal that now the querent needs to put her ideas into action. There may be some testing negotiations ahead; an offer from her manager or a client won't give her much room for maneuver. All she can do here is temper her emotions, and aim to manage difficult people and situations with skill and consideration.

WEEK FOUR: The Four of Cups shows that the querent will feel that her life is back in kilter, but there may also be a trace of irritation or boredom—maybe because issues from week two do not get resolved. This may escalate into a battle, shown by the Three of Swords. Suffering painful disappointment may be the only way to get to the heart of a problem and subsequently resolve it.

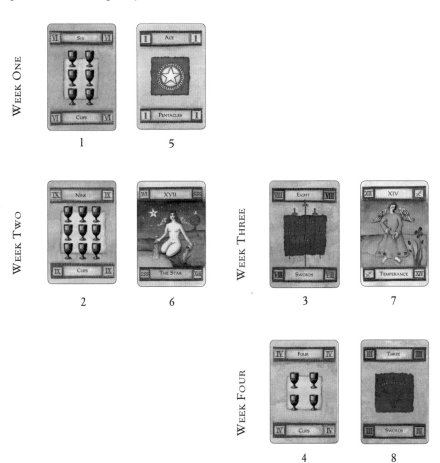

THE WEEK AHEAD SPREAD

This spread is an ideal way to gain insight into an important week ahead. Shuffle and cut the cards as usual, then lay them out following the arrangement shown, beginning with the significator card. Interpret this card first to get a feel for the whole seven days, then interpret each of the other cards in turn.

SAMPLE READING: WHAT THE NEXT WEEK HAS IN STORE

The querent wanted to see how she would prosper financially, creatively, and socially during the week ahead.

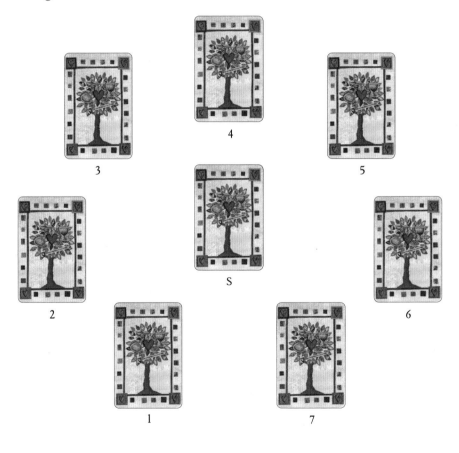

CARD 1: MONDAY   CARD 5: TUESDAY

CARD 2: WEDNESDAY   CARD 6: THURSDAY

CARD 3: FRIDAY   CARD 7: SATURDAY

CARD 4: SUNDAY   S: SIGNIFICATOR CARD

THE SIGNIFICATOR (S): The significator card is the Ten of Wands. This foretells an incredibly busy week; the querent may take on too much and feel overburdened with responsibility (some readers prefer to shuffle and cut the cards again when this card arrives: see page 140). However, the overall outlook—given the spread of cards—is very positive.

MONDAY (1): The Eight of Wands brings great news and happiness. This is an auspicious day for work and expressing her talents.

TUESDAY (5): The Knight of Pentacles reveals that Tuesday is fortuitous for getting things done. It may not be inspiring, but progress is assured.

WEDNESDAY (2): Judgement symbolizes the summing up of a series of events before moving on. It is likely that the querent is coming to the end of a project, and will assess what has been achieved.

3: FRIDAY

4: SUNDAY

5: TUESDAY

2: WEDNESDAY

S: SIGNIFICATOR

6: THURSDAY

1: MONDAY

7: SATURDAY

THURSDAY (6): The Ten of Cups shows great reward and joy, which is usually connected with a community or group of people such as family, friends, or work colleagues. It brings success and achievement, so this is a great day for social gatherings and celebrations.

FRIDAY (3): The Chariot. After the summing up of Wednesday and Thursday's happy endings, Friday sees the querent take up the reins once more to move forward. This should be a day of energy and determined action; the card can also indicate a literal journey, so the querent may take a short trip.

SATURDAY (7): The Three of Cups crowns the sixth day, bringing harmony and love. It shows babies and children; in work terms, this is renewal and the seeds of a new venture. There will be socializing, too.

SUNDAY: (4) The Nine of Cups is the card drawn for Sunday. This Nine is traditionally the "wish" card of the minor arcana (see page 138), so this is a day on which the querent's dreams can come true. She will have the energy to enjoy socializing, so this should be a wonderful day on which she can relax and appreciate all that she has achieved.

What to Do if You Cannot Make Sense of a Reading

If the cards that are first laid out for a reading just don't feel right, and you cannot get into an interpretative flow, bear in mind the following:

1. You can ask the querent to shuffle and cut the deck again. If the first cards are right, some or all of them will reappear in the second reading. This may sound unconvincing, but try this for yourself when you are self-reading and cannot attune to the cards you draw. A sign that reshuffling needs to be done is when the Ten of Wands arises; this often means that there is just too much going on, and you need more time to clear your mind as you reshuffle again.

2. Don't look up the card meanings. Go with your intuitive response to the images—shapes, color, symbols, and mood. Say what you feel, and you will find that the cards open up to you.

3. You may feel hesitant if the cards are "bad": the Tower, the Devil, or Death, for example. Although they might seem traumatic, these cards often signal release and new beginnings. Within each is the gift of action and necessary change. And consider that, for some querents, the opportunity to talk about difficult situations is a release in itself.

4 INTERPRETING THE CARDS
THE MAJOR ARCANA

THE TWENTY-TWO CARDS OF THE MAJOR ARCANA are numbered from 0 to XXI. The sequence can be seen as a quest for self-knowledge; alongside the individual meanings of the cards, the major arcana cards that we draw in a reading are indicative of a stage in our thinking and spiritual development. The Tarot journey begins with card 0, the Fool, and ends with card XXI, the World—beginning again with the reborn Fool: it is a continuous cycle of birth and regeneration. The innocent Fool experiences the other twenty-one cards as landmarks and tests as he seeks completion—the integration of mind, body, and spirit that is symbolized by the World.

THE FOOL'S STORY
DISCOVERY: THE FOOL TO THE CHARIOT

The Fool is zero, an innocent who sets the wheel of the Tarot cycle in motion. He encounters I, the Magician, the alchemist who shows him the magical potential at his fingertips. With the Fool's growing awareness of his environment, he then turns his attention to his earthly and spiritual parents. These are II, the High Priestess—the goddess

aspect of his mother—and III, the Empress, who takes care of his earthly needs. Similarly, his father the Emperor, IV, makes the rules; the Emperor's spiritual counterpart, the Hierophant, V, gives him an education. Card VI, the Lovers, is the first test of the Fool's autonomy, for he must choose between the parental bond and a relationship with a partner. When he meets the Chariot, VII, he realizes his freedom and risks dealing with the world alone.

THE LESSONS: JUSTICE TO TEMPERANCE

The Fool now encounters Justice, VIII (in some decks, numbered XI). He is judged by others and must account for his actions. The Hermit, IX, teaches him how to be alone and seek out what he needs, away from his peers. The Wheel of Fortune, X, takes him out of his ego with the realization that he is at the mercy of the greater power, Fate. In Strength, XI, the Fool learns gentleness when dealing with external opponents and internal conflict, and he must be prepared to make a sacrifice, which is symbolized by card XII, the Hanged Man. Death, XIII, brings both endings and renewal; the transition of spirit. Temperance, XIV, heralds the spiritual alchemist, and so the Fool learns to control his temperament and quantify the elements of his life.

FROM DARKNESS TO LIGHT: THE DEVIL TO THE WORLD

The Fool's darkness is a power struggle between his lower instincts and his higher nature. He meets card XV, the Devil, and so greets temptation: having to choose between greed and generosity, lust and love. His success depends on his maturity. Yet whatever he envisages as being within his control, life has other plans. The Tower of his ego, XVI, collapses to make way for his connection to heavenly inspiration, in the form

of the Star, XVII. Here, he realizes his goals and finds spiritual guidance, which take him to the creative sanctuary of the Sun, XIX. Yet his journey is not yet complete. As the Fool has moved from the twilight of the Star to the full heat of the Sun, so he has had to endure the disillusion of the Moon, XVIII, which exposes his deepest fears. He must again make a difficult decision that will ensure his

progress. Judgement, XX, is the Fool's final calling to judge himself. He knows that his journey is almost complete. He has the World, XXI, to discover, all over again.

ABOVE: *The World, probably dating from fifteenth-century Italy, bears a similarity to the World card of the Visconti-Sforza deck (see page 108).*

A MEDITATION ON THE FIGURE-OF-EIGHT

The figure-of-eight, or lemniscate, appears prominently on two major arcana cards: the Magician and Strength. It is also evident in the Rider Waite Smith deck on the Two of Pentacles and on the crossed arms of the man on the Nine of Cups.

The figure-of-eight is the ancient infinity symbol. It is also a kind of Tarot DNA, because it represents the flow of never-ending energy created by the tension between two opposite poles.

Tarotist Alfred Douglas uses the figure-of-eight as a way to examine the relationships between the cards of the major arcana. The cards are laid out in a figure-of-eight shape (see opposite). The upper loop of cards points outward and the lower loop inward, with the Wheel of Fortune and the World crossing in the center. These cards represent the midpoint and end of the Tarot journey. The upper loop symbolizes the self and our relationship with the outside world; the cards of the lower loop reveal the inner spiritual path.

Each card in the upper loop has a counterpart in the lower loop, which can give the upper-loop card greater context. If you discover a pair of cards in a spread that relate in this way, it can aid your interpretation. For example, the Hermit's counterpart is Strength, who introduces the traditionally feminine quality of gentleness to balance the Hermit's analytical masculinity. Strength is also what the Hermit will need while he is alone in the wilderness.

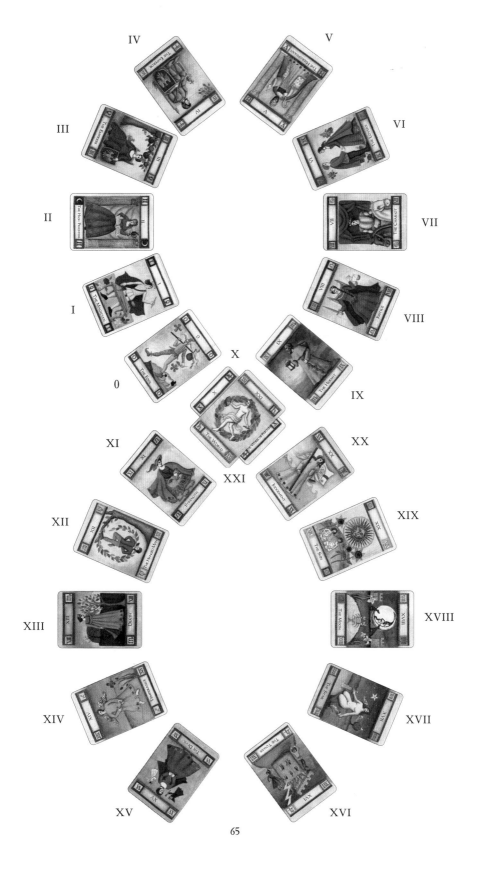

IV

V

III

VI

II

VII

I

VIII

0

X

IX

XI

XXI

XX

XII

XIX

XIII

XVIII

XIV

XVII

XV

XVI

0 THE FOOL

THE JESTER

The Fool is innocence. Poised to leap between one world and another, he risks the spiritual unknown. He appears in Tarots as a beggar, a madman, a naive youth, and a jester. As the court jester can often articulate subtle or difficult truths, so the Tarot Fool may make his entrance into a reading to remind you of the intemperance and absurdity of life. And, as the jester plays off the crowd, so it has been suggested that he is set to experience the collective journey of all the cards in the major arcana cycle.

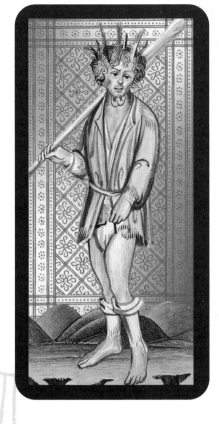

SYMBOLISM

The Visconti-Sforza Fool is depicted as a beggar wearing thin robes; half-dressed, with his britches down, he is a humble, or perhaps humiliated, figure with only his staff to defend or guide him. The seven chicken feathers in his hair symbolize the poverty of his experience as he begins his journey. Tarot historians also assign the Fool as symbol of Lent because he has surrendered his worldly goods. Modern decks show a dog (see page 30) at the Fool's heels, a warning of danger as he is about to step off a precipice. He carries a small bag for a great journey; within it are the four suit objects we see in the Magician, the next card in the sequence. In some decks the Fool carries a flower or is entranced by a butterfly, which act as symbols of his idealism and thirst for discovery. The unnumbered Fool is zero, because his potential is yet to be realized.

ASTROLOGY

The Fool's planet is Uranus, symbolizing independence and freedom. Uranus is named after the Greek god Uranus, "Father Sky," linking with the Fool's element of Air.

Upright Meaning: Beginnings

A fresh start; freedom from the constraints of the past; release from a pattern of events; and taking risks—provided you can enjoy the freefall. With this vital opportunity comes the need for caution, so temper your idealism with practicality. As the jester, he can also herald a beguiling character who brings innocence and fun.

Reversed Meaning: Irresponsibility

In the reversed position, the negative traits of the Fool come to the fore. Naivety turns to immaturity and irresponsibility, warning that a spontaneous decision needs a rethink. A business venture, plans for a new property or a whirlwind relationship may dissolve due to lack of foresight. He may also represent the literal Fool, who turns your world upside down.

Card Combinations

The upright interpretation of the Fool may be modified if he appears as one of the last cards that you lay out in a spread. In this instance he would show the completion of the journey. To reveal whether his appearance is fortuitous or foolish, look at the nature of the surrounding cards in a reading:

THE FOOL WITH THE STAR	THE FOOL WITH THE MOON
An inspired risk; a creative or spiritual quest	Impulsiveness leads to a confidence crisis; action before due thought

I THE MAGICIAN

THE MAGUS

The Magician represents manifestation. In early Tarot decks such as the Visconti-Sforza, he may be seen as a merchant or artisan, whereas later decks show him as the magician, holding up his baton or magic wand. These are the two faces of the Magician: the magus, the channeler of energy to be directed to his will, and the artisan. When reversed, the Magician descends to the traveling charlatan who, through sleight of hand, deceives and mystifies. In Italy, the Magician was originally known as *Il Bagatella*, or "game of tricks."

SYMBOLISM

The Magician weaves magic with the four elements. On his table are the four suit symbols of the minor arcana: Pentacle, Cup, Sword, and Wand; earth, water, air, and fire are at his disposal.

The lemniscate, or figure-of-eight, for infinity (see pages 64–65) shown above his head in modern decks denotes the infinite flow of universal energy. Around his waist is a belt, sometimes referred to as a serpent-girdle, a symbol of alchemy, revealing renewal. The Magician's wand represents manifestation, and the card number is 1, for the individual and primal energy.

ASTROLOGY

The Magician's planet is Mercury, ruler of communication. Also known as Hermes, the winged messenger of Greek myth, Mercury was the Roman god of magic. In its form of quick-silver, mercury is associated with transformation, the essence of magic.

UPRIGHT MEANING: HUMAN MAGIC

You have everything you need at your fingertips to create now whatever you choose. This is a card of communication, a call to action and self-expression. The Magician's charmed influence indicates travel and creative projects, communication and energy. This is an auspicious card for business dealings. You can have what you desire; you just need to see what lies before you and realize your resources. Start with one telephone call or email, and everything else can align, as if by magic.

REVERSED MEANING: TRICKERY

The Magician reversed warns of cheating and false appearances, dreams without foundation, and even self-delusion. A situation or individual is not what you think. For artists and entrepreneurs, he can represent a creative block.

CARD COMBINATIONS

It is helpful to take note of the minor arcana cards that appear with the Magician in a reading. Because he has the four suit emblems before him, the suit or suits that surround him can reveal the way in which his influence will be expressed:

THE MAGICIAN WITH THE ACE OF PENTACLES	THE MAGICIAN WITH THE QUEEN OF CUPS
New financial opportunities; prosperity; establishment	New relationships; a relationship moves forward; happiness

II THE HIGH PRIESTESS

THE PAPESS

The High Priestess is the archetype of mystic femininity, the keeper of wisdom that is not easily expressed. She is not of words, but of experience, intuition, and dreams. She represents learning and mediation between opposites. In a reading, her appearance guides you to listen to your inner voice in order to move forward. She is the natural counterpart of card V, the Hierophant, but her earthly expression can be seen in the next card in the sequence, the Empress, or Mother Earth.

SYMBOLISM

The High Priestess holds a book and sometimes a pomegranate or flower, symbols of her developed learning. The book, or scroll depicted in some decks, represents the Torah, Judaism's sacred book of wisdom. In modern decks, the veil behind her shows that she is in touch with unconscious and conscious feelings. The two pillars (opposite) are from the Tree of Life. On the Rider Waite Smith deck, they bear a B on the left-hand pillar and a J on the right. These

initials stand for Boaz, representing the elements of Water and Earth, and Jachin, for Fire and Air. Boaz and Jachin are names on the pillars in Solomon's Temple that relate to kabbalistic Tarot (see page 24). The two pillars also reflect her number, II, revealing the balance and opposition of co-dependent elements.

ASTROLOGY

The Moon is the planet of the High Priestess, signifying the inner world of secrets, emotion, and hidden knowledge. The waxing and waning moons link her with feminine, cyclic nature. The crescent moon represents expansion, the waning moon decline.

UPRIGHT MEANING: INTUITION

Higher guidance. Take note of your dreams; nurture your desire for learning and seek out inspiration. In this aspect, the High Priestess is the teaching of your intuition. The duality of her number, II, may also indicate the need to choose between two courses of action. Take time to make this decision; listen to those who have the appropriate wisdom and experience. Their words are genuine, and may help you heal a private conflict before it becomes a moral dilemma.

REVERSED MEANING: SECRETS REVEALED

In this position, the High Priestess shows that a secret is about to be revealed. With this, emotions surface and you may discover that your faith has been misplaced. A trusted authority figure, such as a spiritual advisor, educator, or manager, fails you by giving you wrong information or a wrong impression. An additional meaning is feeling disconnected from your inner knowledge.

CARD COMBINATIONS

With the Moon, a confidence crisis concerning a woman is revealed, or the need for intuitive guidance to make a key decision. With the Hanged Man, a spiritual perspective changes your viewpoint and calls for time away from a situation.

THE FEMALE POPE

In the Visconti-Sforza deck, the High Priestess was thought to have been painted in the likeness of Sister Manfreda, a relative of the Visconti family of northern Italy who commissioned a set of cards to commemorate the marriage of Bianca-Maria Visconti and Francesco Sforza in 1441 (see page 9). Sister Manfreda (Maifreda da Pirovano) was a member of a Gnostic sect, the Guglielmites, and, according to some sources, a nun of the Order of the Humiliati. The High Priestess may be wearing the habit of the Order, who were famous in western Europe for their wool cloth.

The Guglielmites were founded by a woman, Guglielma of Bohemia (d. 1281), and inspired by the prophecies of a twelfth-century Calabrian abbot, Joachim da Fiore. The sect believed that Christ would return in the year 1300, heralding a new age in which women could take the mantle of Pope. In readiness, Sister Manfreda was chosen as the first female Pope, when she would officiate a mass at Santa Maria Maggiore, Rome. However, before she could fulfill her unorthodox calling she was burned at the stake for heresy in late 1300.

III The Empress

The Empress is Mother Earth. Serene and full-figured, she represents fulfilled potential: close and happy relationships, nurturing, and abundance. She is a goddess of love in human form, and all benefit from her magnanimity. She expresses herself through dialogue and her relationships with others. Whereas the High Priestess is the private, intuitive aspect of femininity, the Empress is the material aspect whose creativity is expressed through her children and consort, the Emperor, and her connection to nature.

Symbolism

The eagle, the masculine protection symbol on her shield, is the emblem of the Roman Empire that appears on the Emperor card.

Birds are also symbols of the soul so the eagle reveals the Empress as the essence, or soul, of the Earth. The Empress's hands are green (see page 31)—the green fingers that make the garden grow. In the Visconti-Sforza deck the Empress is crowned, which in later esoteric decks such as the Rider Waite Smith and Sacred Rose is transformed into a diadem of twelve stars. This represents the twelve signs of the zodiac and months of the year. In *The Magic of Tarot* (see opposite), the apple denotes female sexuality, linking her to biblical Eve, who chose knowledge of life over perfection. The apple tree symbolizes an abundance of giving and receiving. The Empress's number is dynamic III, representing the triad of creation: mother, father, child.

Astrology

The Empress is associated with Venus, planet of love and fertility. Venus is concerned with what you value—relationships, material comfort, sensuousness, and sensitivity.

THE EARTH MOTHER AND THE APPLE

The Tarot's Empress is the Great Mother, or mother-goddess, worshipped by many cultures as a symbol of divine creativity and earthly fertility. The Empress's planet, Venus, is also the Roman goddess of sexuality and love, revered as Aphrodite in ancient Greece and as Demeter, meaning "mother earth" or "grain mother." In Egypt the mother-goddesses were Isis and Hathor, who were linked with the cow-goddess Mehet-Weret who brought the Inundation of the Nile and with it the survival of crops. In folklore, apples (see *The Magic of Tarot* card, below) were once used in love divination, in the game of apple-bobbing or apple-ducking. On Hallowe'en, apples were floated in water or tied on a string. Holding their hands behind their backs—and sometimes blindfolded—villagers attempted to bite an apple. If a single woman succeeded, she placed her apple under her pillow, and it is said she would dream of her future husband that night.

UPRIGHT MEANING: ABUNDANCE

Giving and receiving love comes naturally; money comes, bringing material comforts. You are supported and cherished, and can give to others unconditionally. The Empress can also predict a new relationship or a pregnancy, and the positive influence of a mother-figure, as well as fertile ideas; this is an auspicious time to nurture new creative projects. Ultimately, the upright Empress is a card of reassurance; know that you will grow and not falter in whatever you choose to do.

REVERSED MEANING: INSECURITY

Mothering becomes smothering when the Empress turns. Domestic bliss turns to chaos, so this card can reveal unhappiness at home. The thrust of the reversed Empress is scarcity rather than abundance, so you may feel that you can never have enough of what you need to sustain you—affection, money, and support. The root of this may be a mother-figure who is negative, controlling, or undermining. Additional meanings include fertility issues, creative blocks, and a need for personal validation.

CARD COMBINATIONS

With the Ace of Cups, a relationship or pregnancy that brings happiness is revealed. With Temperance, the needs of a family may be a source of tension.

IV The Emperor

The Emperor represents order and authority. His qualities are traditionally masculine: martialism (in some decks he wears a suit of silver armor), rationalism, and virility. He can be depicted in a desert; the lack of water, which symbolizes the emotions, establishes that reason, not feeling, rules him. His natural consort, the Empress, represents love, whereas the Emperor reveals power. In this sense, he can be perceived as uninspiring or oppressive, a law-maker. Yet the Emperor also deals in the immediate present, taking what is before him at face value. In this sense, he heralds a time when we must deal with practicalities.

Symbolism

The Emperor sits upright, in ready defence of the realm, sometimes holding an orb and scepter or wand. His shield shows earthly stability, and is emblazoned with the insignia of the black eagle, which denotes protection and masculine energy. His throne symbolizes ultimate stability. In the Visconti-Sforza deck, the Emperor wears the ducal family crown, which is shown with decorative foliage. His number, IV, is the number of structure and civilization. On early cards such as the Cary-Yale Visconti-Sforza, the Emperor is surrounded by four pages, who bear allegiance to his rulership. His white beard represents wisdom.

Astrology

The Emperor's sign is Aries, the Ram. Aries is ruled by Mars, a reminder of the Emperor's martial qualities as a defender of his kingdom.

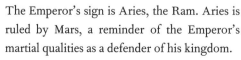

Upright Meaning: Fatherhood, Protection

The help of a father-figure, paternal love, and protection. This man will act, not pontificate, so his influence in a reading can reveal a life partner, guardian or parent, or someone in your life with wisdom and ambition. He is also a natural rule-maker; as a parent, he sets the boundaries, so his appearance in a reading can show a requirement to conform. For women and men, the Emperor can predict a partner. More generally, the card denotes a return to order after a period of uncertainty.

Reversed Meaning: Oppression

The reversed Emperor is deliberating and stubborn. He is more interested in controlling than supporting you, and his love of convention here turns to oppression, overruling your needs or ideas. The reversed Emperor can therefore predict problems with parental or other authority figures. Overall, the card can indicate disorder and a need for structure and organization.

Card Combinations

With the Magician, there is focused creativity as ideas take a workable form.
With the Fool, a man with status brings adventure.
With Strength, the Emperor brings further security.

THE BLACK EAGLE AND THE EMPEROR

The imperial black eagle officially became an insignia of the Visconti family (see page 9) in 1397, two years after Gian Galeazzo Visconti had bought himself the hereditary title of Duke of Milan. Gian Galeazzo had deposed his uncle Bernabo in 1385 to take power, and the family's prominence grew as it ruled over much of northern Italy. In 1395, Gian Galeazzo purchased his title from Emperor Wenceslas of Germany. The newly created dukedom formed a part of the Roman Empire, which granted the use of the black eagle to the Viscontis. In the Visconti-Sforza Tarot, the Emperor wears the symbol of the black eagle on his hat; the card may represent Emperor Wenceslas, although there are numerous theories regarding his original identity. In the Ancient Italian Tarot (1880), the eagle appears as an emblem on the Empress's shield, whereas on the Emperor card the eagle is a living creature, poised to protect the domain of the Emperor, who rests his left arm on the creature's head, emphasizing greater male, and specifically paternal, power.

V THE HIEROPHANT

THE HIGH PRIEST, THE POPE

The Hierophant is the upholder of spiritual tradition. His natural counterpart is card II, the High Priestess; the High Priestess works in secret, whereas the Hierophant works in public, mediating beween Earth and heaven, offering spiritual counsel. The Hierophant may appear as an orthodox Catholic, but in a reading, he represents the nature of our individual faith and the quest for oneness.

SYMBOLISM

The Hierophant wears a triple crown which, with his crook or scepter, stands for religious authority. He makes the gesture of Papal benediction; in some early decks, the Hierophant is named Pope. Tarots often depict him standing between two pillars, with two acolytes before him and a pair of crossed keys by his feet. The pillars denote knowledge while the keys—which are the keys to the kingdom of heaven—symbolize spiritual authority. Numbered V, the number of mankind, the Hierophant arbitrates the relationship between man and God. Five also represents the card's meaning of unity, as five is indivisible by any number other than one.

ASTROLOGY

The sign associated with the Hierophant or Pope is Taurus, the symbol of which is the Bull. A papal law or edict may also be referred to as a papal bull.

UPRIGHT MEANING: GROWTH

In the upright position, the Hierophant foretells teaching, spiritual advancement, and unity. Divine inspiration is available to you—in the detail of everyday life, in the order of nature that is universally shared. This card shows you the sanctuary of a community, particularly in relation to education, such as a study group. For individuals, the Hierophant can take the form of a teacher-angel who watches over you from above. In some instances, the Hierophant as priest can also predict a partnership or marriage.

REVERSED MEANING: RESTRICTION

When the Hierophant is in the reversed position, misinformation or a drive for unreasonable or unattainable perfection is revealed. Restrictive attitudes and the lack of a free flow of ideas casts suspicion and creates an atmosphere of mistrust. The Hierophant reversed can therefore manifest as an organizational crisis at work or, for individuals, criticism that blocks projects. During this confusing influence, make a vow to motivate yourself with achievable goals that you alone appreciate and define.

CARD COMBINATIONS

It can be helpful to think of the Hierophant broadly as a symbol of tradition, unity, and self-development. Compare his qualities with those of the other cards that surround him.

THE HIEROPHANT WITH
THE TEN OF WANDS
Feeling oppressed by
authority/conformity

THE HIEROPHANT WITH
THE LOVERS
Partnerships and commitment; love
and marriage

 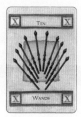  

VI The Lovers

The Lovers depicts a meeting of two hearts. In a garden paradise, the lovers are on the threshold of commitment. A decision is coming: the right decision can secure long-term happiness and gain, and this choice can relate to any situation as well as a love relationship. This is a turning point on the path, and the choices made now can have a profound and positive impact on the future. For this reason, the lovers are shown in an idealized situation, blissfully unaware of what lies ahead.

Symbolism

In the Visconti-Sforza deck (above), the two figures have been identified as Bianca-Maria Visconti and Francesco Sforza (see page 9). The robes of both figures are decorated with suns and rays, the heraldic devices of the two families. The female figure wears a green glove, symbol of love and fertility, and Cupid appears above the couple, poised to release his arrow. On modern Tarots we see a variation of this image, sometimes with Archangel Raphael presiding rather than Cupid. In *The Magic of Tarot* (below and opposite), the flowers represent growth. The card's number, VI, symbolizes harmony.

THE LOVERS AND
THE ACE OF CUPS
Falling in love; marriage,
pregnancy

ASTROLOGY

The sign of the Lovers is Gemini, the Twins. As the twins gaze at each other in union, so too they can turn away from commitment.

UPRIGHT MEANING: A DECISION

An opportunity to move on, but in order to do so an essential decision needs to be made. This often concerns the past and the future, in terms of letting go of one life phase to welcome the new. In families, this may concern duty to a relative that compromises a relationship. When this card appears in a reading you go for what you want and consequently energy and vision are your rewards. In this sense, the Lovers is about commitment to love itself and for yourself, not just love for an individual.

REVERSED MEANING: AVOIDANCE

When the Lovers invert, you go for the easy option, the path of least resistance, which gets you out of a troublesome situation. This, however, is temporary and takes you no further forward in your relationships or goals. Another meaning of this card is temptation and possible betrayal, in the sense that you undervalue your needs; this card may also reveal an emotional betrayal by a partner, but more often a failure of nerve to make a mature decision.

CARD COMBINATIONS

When surrounded by positive cards, the Lovers reveals that you make the right decision regarding a relationship. When negative cards are close by, you take the path of least resistance that leaves important issues unresolved.

THE LOVERS AND THE DEVIL
A decision that leads to entrapment
or lack of fulfillment

THE LOVERS AND THE CHARIOT
A positive choice brings progress,
energy, and/or travel

VII The Chariot

The charioteer represents energy and progress. With the previous card, the Lovers, a decision was made; the Chariot can therefore be interpreted as the resulting action of this choice. Life drives forward, and the charioteer must show steady purpose to gain the valuable experience that this journey offers and find his or her destination. He or she can be likened to the Roman charioteer who parades in victory; however, in his triumph he must also rein in his ego.

Symbolism

The charioteer is male in many decks, but the Visconti-Sforza deck depicts a woman, dressed in similar style to that of the female lover on card VI; she may represent Bianca-Maria Visconti (see page 9). The winged horses (or sphinxes) symbolize instinct and speed, which the charioteer must harness; if the horses run wild, he or she loses balance. The rider has no reins, so controls the animals through sheer force of will. In later decks the horses are often black and white, signifying the dark and light aspects of the charioteer's journey and the light and shadow aspects of his or her personality. Numbered VII, this card combines the action of three with the stability of four, which represents moving onward from a strong position; VII may also represent the sum of the four-wheeled chariot, two horses, and charioteer.

Astrology

The Chariot is associated with emotional Cancer, the Crab. Like the Crab with his hard shell and soft center, he must balance his head and heart in order to move forward.

Upright Meaning: Progress

When the Chariot appears in your reading, action is the key word. Events are about to speed up and success is within reach. The card reveals movement in terms of a journey, yet often denotes another kind of departure from the familiar to the unknown—new work, a new location, moving on from (or growing closer in) a long-term relationship, or making significant progress in a creative or business project. To stay true to your path, approach this situation with drive, focus, and determination, but keep in balance. This is a chance to take control, succeed, and break down barriers. When you get where you want to be, appreciate the gifts you gain. An additional meaning is more literal: driving a car or purchasing a new vehicle.

Reversed Meaning: Frustration

The Chariot reversed is an arrogant charioteer, expecting unqualified support from

those around him. Ego is in the way; this may be a reflection of your attitude, or you suffer due to others' egomania. On a literal level, the upturned Chariot reveals delayed travel and unexpected obstacles barring your path. Well-intentioned plans gone awry may lead you to believe that you have made a mistake. One way to get through the influence of this card is to switch your focus and if necessary, begin again.

Card Combinations

With Justice, a journey is morally justified; an outcome in your favor brings freedom.
With Judgement, an era is near its end, and a new phase in life beckons.

The Chariot as the Persona

In kabbala, each Tarot trump has an associated Hebrew letter and a correspondence on the Tree of Life (see page 26). In this system, the Chariot takes the letter chet (heth), meaning fence or enclosure. This enclosure is the chariot itself, which is a metaphor for the shell of the personality that protects our vulnerability. However, at some point the shell can become restrictive and must be expanded or discarded, just as the developing personality must adapt to fit one's circumstances. In this sense, the charioteer's challenge is growth and movement that is consistent with his purpose.

VIII JUSTICE

THE SCALES

After the Chariot comes Justice, who judges the charioteer's past actions. Justice represents decisions, righting previous wrongs, and restoring balance. Along with legal rulings, Justice also encompasses any situation in which we are assessed or judged by others.

SYMBOLISM

Justice carries the traditional objects of her craft, the scales of mercy and the sword of retribution or protection. Justice's sword, like the suit of Swords in the minor arcana, represents logic and the mind. On the Visconti-Sforza card (right), a knight on a white steed flies over the the figure of Justice, sword in hand, denoting speed, action, and conclusions. Justice here is outdoors, perhaps indicating that her work is public; in later Tarots she is often shown inside, also seated on a throne of authority, in what may be imagined a public courtroom or chamber.

ASTROLOGY

Justice is associated with Libra, the Scales. The Scales represent evaluation, fairness, and balance.

LEGAL DEITIES

Justice is one of three virtue cards in standard Tarot decks, along with Strength (card XI or VIII) and Temperance (XIV). The personification of justice as female dates to classical antiquity and the Greek goddess Themis (the Roman Justitia), deity of divine law; and Dike, Themis's daughter, who concerned herself with human law.

Dike is depicted with scales, while Themis and Justitia are depicted in classical statuary with both sword and scales. As with Tarot's Justice, these deities are shown without blindfolds—so Tarot's Justice card evokes their early representations, before the fifteenth century, after which artists began to show Justice wearing a blindfold.

The scales signify the weighing of evidence, and the sword, the legal ruling. The sword therefore may demand retribution from, or give protection to, the defendant. The scales can be seen as the feminine—the receiving of evidence into a circular scale—and the sword, masculinity, the external expression of the internal process of decision-making as a straight line. Justice holds both in perfect balance.

UPRIGHT MEANING: RESOLUTION

A legal matter is resolved. This is justice in its truest sense, because it takes no heed of your position. Therefore, the appearance of Justice may be a card of satisfaction or discomfort, depending on your circumstances; the truth is that a final decision is made that must be accepted. Taken positively, Justice in the upright position legitimizes an endeavor and predicts success in business and legal dealings. An additional meaning is divine law—guidance and direction from a spiritual source.

REVERSED MEANING: INJUSTICE

When reversed, Justice becomes a miscarriage of justice. You will know that you are right, yet the system goes against you. What you believe to be the truth is manipulated by others who are less qualified to fight your case. Fend off others' lack of faith and protect your integrity; choose new representatives or partners in business.

CARD COMBINATIONS

With Judgement, the practical and spiritual outcome of a situation.
With the Wheel of Fortune, a resolution brings freedom.

IX The Hermit

Time

The Hermit is the seeker of knowledge. Often depicted wearing the habit of a monk, he chooses a lone path away from familiar comfort in order to pursue a personal quest. He is solitary rather than lonely, as his moving away from society is his choice. He embraces nature as a way to heal himself and is guided by the light of his inner strength. When he appears in a reading, he brings a quieter pace of life; time slows down.

Symbolism

The Visconti-Sforza Hermit (right) holds an hourglass, a reference to his secondary title of Time; an aged man, his beard denotes the wisdom of experience. In later decks (see *The Magic of Tarot*, opposite), the Hermit holds a lit lantern, representing inner guidance, and carries a staff encircled by a snake in the form of the symbol of Asclepius, the ancient Greek god of healing. The darkness around him suggests a spiritual wilderness as he strives to find inner truth. His number, IX, comprises three triads, representing the integration of mind, body, and spirit.

THE HERMIT WITH THE STAR
A time of withdrawal that leads to inspiration and creativity

THE HERMIT WITH DEATH
A new way of thinking; a quiet, positive time after the trauma of change

ASTROLOGY

The Hermit's sign is Virgo, the Virgin. In this sense the Hermit is linked with card II, the virginal High Priestess, who also seeks and holds knowledge that is hidden.

UPRIGHT MEANING: THE JOURNEY

The Hermit can reveal a need for reflection, healing, and discovery. You have to rely upon yourself, but you have the resourcefulness and integrity to find your way. This is an important card for self-knowledge and inner strength. It can reveal a physical or inner journey that will bring emotional reward and spiritual learning. The appearance of the Hermit in a reading also relates to needing more time—to go at a pace that allows you to think clearly. An additional meaning is meditation.

REVERSED MEANING: ISOLATION

The Hermit reversed reveals isolation that is imposed rather than chosen. You may be cut off from your usual support systems or feel cast out by a community; in this context, the lone Hermit is sad and world-weary. This is circumstantial, however, and the isolation temporary. Bear in mind that this card can also be a reflection of your fear of being rejected by others. As the upright Hermit needs time to consider and reflect, so in the reversed position there is intransigence. Stubbornness or rash reactions, rather than thought, may see this Hermit lose his way in the wilderness.

CARD COMBINATIONS

When interpreting the Hermit with other cards, you may like to consider issues of time. With the Hermit, time slows down, whereas the Aces and Knights of the more physically active suits (Wands and Swords) generally show that events will speed up. For example, the Hermit combined with the Knight of Wands would reveal a time of rest followed by intense activity.

THE HERMIT WITH
THE ACE OF PENTACLES
Renewed energy; a new beginning
after a time of healing

X The Wheel of Fortune

Fate

The Wheel of Fortune marks the halfway stage in the cycle of the major arcana. After the soul-searching Hermit, the Wheel brings a new lesson—we get to understand Fate, to see what we can, and cannot, control, and go with its flow. In Buddhism, this may be thought of as an understanding of non-attachment. We may explore our own psyches, but we cannot control the greater workings of the universe.

Symbolism

The Visconti-Sforza deck shows a wheel with the figure of Fortune. Around her are four figures that represent rising and falling fortunes—the aged beggar, two youths, and a small figure with the ears of an ass, for foolishness—as if man could ever have a say in his own destiny. Many later decks portray animals representing this cycle (see opposite). The monkey is vanity and impermanence; the ass is humility and human error; the dragon, the primal energy of nature. The dragon brandishes a sword, like the figure of Justice, card VIII. With the turning of the wheel, we need to be ready to see and experience life from all sides. In Buddhism, the wheel is a symbol of *dharma*, the Buddha's teachings. This card is numbered X, which signifies completeness.

Astrology

The Wheel of Fortune card is associated with Jupiter, the planet linked with luck and learning.

UPRIGHT MEANING: A TURN FOR THE BETTER

The Wheel heralds an improvement in your circumstances. Be open to change and new knowledge, and accept the gifts that life brings. Good fortune awaits; anything is possible. Spiritually, this card can reveal that there is a whole side of life you have not yet experienced, along with a calling to psychic or spiritual development work.

REVERSED MEANING: CLOSURE

Unlike many reversed cards, the Wheel is not negative. The workings of the universe may be beyond your influence, but the focus is on how you respond to the changes it brings about. You may have difficulty adapting if you feel that the wheel has turned against you, but it is important to accept your situation. Thankfully, the Wheel reversed also foretells closure, the ending of one cycle of destiny. This may bring welcome relief.

CARD COMBINATIONS

The Wheel of Fortune indicates change, usually for the better. The cards that follow the Wheel reveal in which areas of your life this turn of events will be most keenly felt.

THE WHEEL OF FORTUNE WITH
THE MOON (right)
A twist of fate brings about a crisis of confidence; a delay in adapting to altered circumstances

THE WHEEL OF FORTUNE WITH
JUDGEMENT (left)
Events that accidentally work in your favor; synchronicity that quickly concludes important business

XI STRENGTH

FORTITUDE

After Justice, Strength (or Fortitude) is the second of the cardinal virtues to appear in the major arcana sequence (Temperance is the third). Strength is a lesson in dealing with dangerous forces—an internal conflict, or an external enemy—and exerting self-control. This calls for strength of character, a need to integrate the base and higher aspects of our personalities.

SYMBOLISM

The lion symbolizes primal instinct that has to be tamed. In the Visconti-Sforza deck (above), a muscular figure wields a club over the cowed animal. He uses a club rather than a sword, perhaps aiming to subdue the lion rather than kill it. The lion here has an almost human face; Strength is also concerned with taming one's own baser nature. In later decks, the lion is paired with a gentrified lady, who represents civilized society—the animal side of human nature meeting the higher self. Her hat makes the shape of a lazy eight, the lemniscate, which is also the Magician's insignia (see page 68). The card's number, when represented as 11 (XI), denotes balance—two equal 1s. The card can be numbered VIII, again signifying balance, comprising two stable 4s.

ASTROLOGY

Strength is associated with Leo, the Lion. In alchemy, the lion is a symbol of primary matter that can be transformed into gold, a metaphor for an enlightened state of mind.

Upright Meaning: Tension

In the upright position, this card signifies the need for patience to deal with passionate forces that may be overwhelming. These may be from within—the lion can reveal that you are fighting your own shadow. Taming the lion, however, is not about takeover, but about self-control and courage when dealing with a challenging situation or fierce impulse. In a reading, Strength also shows that compassion is the way to deal with a person whose outlook is very different from your own. It says, too, that feminine and masculine qualities can come together to create balance. Patience, not force, is the solution. An additional meaning is well-being, and energy and physical strength.

Reversed Meaning: Avoidable Danger

The negative in this card is not the lion, but a fear of the lion. Strength reversed can be interpreted as a weakness of will and an inability to take a genuine risk; rather than deal with discomfiting tension as you work out how to resolve a conflict, you try to deny the enemy all together. This may be the enemy within, when you don't want to listen to your gut instinct for fear of what action you may need to take. The message here is not to panic, nor retreat.

Card Combinations

The Strength card is advice in itself, but when combined with other cards, it enables you to discover more about the nature of a test: this may be a test of will, a moral question, or inner conflict with your conscience or with your head and heart.

STRENGTH WITH THE HANGED MAN	STRENGTH WITH THE FOOL
An ongoing test of will that leads to a sacrifice or change of perspective	An attempt to resolve an issue, opting for escape rather than resolution

XII THE HANGED MAN

THE TRAITOR

The Hanged Man is a seeker of spiritual knowledge. Hanging upside down from a scaffold or tree, he is reminiscent of Odin, the Norse god who discovered the secrets of the runes by suspending himself from the World Tree for nine days and nights. The Hanged Man's peaceful expression reveals his confidence in his predicament. He is safely held while he takes time to see the world from an altered perspective.

SYMBOLISM

In esoteric Tarot, the tree is the Tree of Life, which is central to kabbala (see page 24). The protective garland of leaves that encircles him (see opposite) is open-ended, which indicates that he still has much to accomplish on his journey through the major arcana; the full circle, symbolizing completion, is depicted as a garland on the World, the final card of beginnings and endings (see page 108). The Hanged Man's left foot is safely tethered to the branch of the tree, which shows that the universe will support him. He does not need to cling to the tree, but simply to await the insights that his stance will afford him. The Hanged Man is numbered XII, which represents wholeness and perfection.

ASTROLOGY

The Hanged Man is associated with the planet Neptune. Neptune is the planet of fantasy, dreams, spirituality, imagination, and creativity.

UPRIGHT MEANING: A CHANGE OF PERSPECTIVE

Waiting time; a period of suspension. Use this chosen or enforced delay to look at your circumstances another way. You may need to make a compromise or sacrifice to move forward and find solutions to immediate problems, if your new-found view on the situation requires it. Tarotist Alfred Douglas writes that the Hanged Man reveals a reversal of values, so an unorthodox solution to a problem may present itself. At a spiritual level, the Hanged Man can reveal a period of introspection, a time for spiritual development, guidance, and meditation.

REVERSED MEANING: WASTING TIME

You may think that you are tied to one course of action, or feel you have become martyred to others' demands. Guidance from your unconscious and an openness to look at alternatives will liberate you—an unrealistic fantasy will only bind you more tightly. Release yourself from a contract with others or with yourself that cannot be fulfilled.

CARD COMBINATIONS

With the Hermit, time out for study or self-examination is revealed.
With Death, a final resolution after a period of delay.

THE IDENTITY OF THE HANGED MAN

An alternative name for the Hanged Man is the Traitor, which is the title of the card in Etteilla decks (see page 16). The Hanged Man in the Visconti-Sforza Tarot may portray Muzio Attendolo, a *condottiere* or mercenary (1369–1424), who was father to Francesco Sforza, ruler of Milan (see page 9). During the Hundred Years War, Attendolo helped Gian Galeazzo Visconti defeat the Della Scala family and for his heroism was dubbed *sforza*, or "strength." In 1409 Attendolo killed the tyrant Ottobuono Terzo, an enemy of the Pope, but trouble came when he complained that Pope John had not paid him for services rendered, and changed sides to fight for King Ladislaus of Naples. According to the scholar Geoffrey Trease, the Pope was so angered by Sforza's defection that he commissioned paintings of him as a traitor, hanging by one foot.

XIII DEATH

THE SKELETON

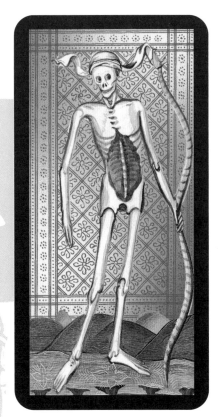

Death is the card of endings and transition. After him comes the Angel of Temperance, card XIV, followed by XV, the Devil, or the light of spirit (the higher self) and the darkness of earth (the base self). Death is interpreted in Tarot as deep change rather than physical death: the definitive—and necessary—ending of a phase or era, so that we may be released to move forward into the future. When Death's influence is done, we can embrace new beginnings expressed in cards such as 0, the Fool and I, the Magician.

SYMBOLISM

In the Visconti-Sforza deck (right), Death is a skeleton-archer who holds what appears to be vertebrae or a snakelike rope in his left hand, and sometimes with a slim arrow in his right. It is likely that the vertebrae are part of a bow; like Cupid (or love), Death strikes at random. While many Tarots do depict Death as a skeleton, there are other interpretations, one of which is shown opposite. Here, the sun is going down on an old way of living, and dead trees recede to make way for new growth. The number of the card is XIII, today still thought of as an unlucky number. Its sum is four (three plus one). Four is the number of stability, representing the aftermath and return to order that follows Death's upheaval. On the Rider Waite Smith Death card, the skeleton on horseback holds a banner that bears the symbol of the rose, which symbolizes renewal.

ASTROLOGY

Death is associated with the sign of Scorpio, the Scorpion. Scorpio is linked with sex and death, the ultimate in beginnings and endings—the dual message of the Death card.

Upright Meaning: Endings

The natural ending of one cycle of destiny; a moving away from old familiar patterns toward new opportunities. The card represents major life changes, such as relocation to a new home or job, the final end of a relationship, or the discarding of old beliefs and values. Remember that this transition is necessary to enable you to move on.

Reversed Meaning: Unexpected Change

Death reversed may occur in a reading to show you that it is time to let go. You may have been holding on to outdated information or a relationship that you are continuing for the sake of it, although it is not fulfilling. If you cannot make the decision right now, this card indicates that change may be made for you. In this sense, Death reversed reveals unexpected events: take this card as an opportunity to prepare yourself.

Card Combinations

At its simplest level, Death shows change, so the surrounding cards help illuminate the nature of that change. Here, Death is in the present position in a spread, and the card to its right represents the future.

Death with the
Hierophant (right)
A spiritual beginning; the comfort of
religion; Karmic lessons

Death with the Lovers (left)
Leaving an established relationship or
lifestyle for a new passion

XIV
TEMPERANCE

Temperance is the third cardinal virtue in the major arcana sequence, along with Justice and Strength (see pages 82, 88). A maiden or an angel pours water from one cup or urn to another. She is a spiritual alchemist, integrating and harmonizing the varied essences of life. Temperance indicates resources, management, and tests—and the need to balance conflicting demands on our time.

SYMBOLISM

The angel or maiden on the card is the Angel of Time, who presides over the past and the future and through whom emotions flow, symbolized by the water. On some decks, the angel has one foot in the pool, the other on land. This represents a striving for balance by careful management of temperamental factors. The irises growing by the water are named after Iris, the Greek rainbow-goddess who brought messages to Earth from the sky-god, Zeus. Iris's symbol is the rainbow, a signifier of hope that appears in contemporary decks. The number of Temperance is XIV, for resolutions and growth.

ASTROLOGY

Temperance is associated with Sagittarius, the Archer or Centaur. The glyph for Sagittarius is the arrow. On the Temperance card, water from the higher urn must be poured at a precise angle to fill the lower; in the same way must the archer have true aim.

UPRIGHT MEANING: RECONCILIATION

You may need to approach a challenging situation with scientific precision. It takes concentration to get the formula right when life feels like a continual balancing act with all its demands on your time. Success, however, requires commitment and effort. The card also suggests reconciliation, the resolving of financial issues, and spiritual guidance.

REVERSED MEANING: IMBALANCE

Temperance reversed indicates a tidal wave of trouble. This manifests as imbalance—past events may threaten to overwhelm you as your usual focus on the present dissolves. This card can also signify poor financial management or a general lack of resources. In love, difficult memories may surface, which may restrict a current relationship. Attention to detail is the best way out of the whirlpool; you are dealing with sensitive issues.

CARD COMBINATIONS

With the Four of Swords, recuperation after a stressful time.
With the World, hard work brings deserved reward.

TAROT ANGELS

Angels traditionally appear on the Lovers, Judgement, and Temperance cards. On Temperance, the angel has been identified as Archangel Michael; on the Lovers, Archangel Raphael, while on the Judgement card, Archangel Gabriel calls us to evaluate our past actions. Angels appear on these three cards because they suggest a need for personal integrity: there is much at stake. Temperance's Archangel Gabriel is ruler of the element of water. Water represents emotion, communication, renewal, and life. If we pay close attention to the demands upon our time rather than being overwhelmed by them, we become active rather than reactive. As the angel manages the flow of water from one cup to another, we too can find the perfect balance.

XV The Devil

Tarot cards often depict the Devil as Satan enslaving a male and female demon. One origin of the Devil is Pan, Greek god of excess (rather than evil). As the Angel of Temperance represents the potential of the higher self, the Devil represents the extremes of the base, or lower, self. When the Devil appears, a decision must be made between our base instincts—fear, lust, greed—and our higher natures.

SYMBOLISM

In the Visconti-Sforza Tarot (right), the Devil is a horned and winged beast who holds two naked figures in his mouth—one male, one female—as if to devour them. His hind legs appear to be reversed; the human figure depicted below the Devil's head symbolizes human oppression. A modern interpretation is shown opposite: a central figure appears with an angel of conscience on one shoulder and a devil of temptation on the other. Both are figments of the imagination, and reveal the Devil's meaning as the conflict of opposing internal forces. In the Rider Waite Smith deck, an inverted pentagram appears, signifying chaos. It may be a representation of the Devil's head; his beard is the lowest point of the pentagram, with his ears and horns associated with the middle and upper pairs of points that constitute the form. His number is XV, which in numerology reduces to six: five plus one. This is the number of the Lovers, which also shows two figures and reveals that a vital choice must be made.

THE DEVIL WITH THE SIX OF CUPS
A choice between love and security
or eroticism and excitement

Astrology

The Devil's astrological sign is Capricorn, the Goat. Capricorn is ruled by Saturn, planet of time and restriction.

Upright Meaning: Temptation

The Devil indicates temptation and obligation. The card reveals painful lessons: addiction, affairs, a moral debt, or other restriction, such as employment with little reward. At any point, however, you can choose to walk away; it is, after all, a situation that you may have created. The Devil urges you to make a mature choice that will bring long-term benefits to your life, rather than short-term gratification.

Reversed Meaning: Enslavement

The upright meaning of the Devil is intensified in the reversed position. Here, the sense of temptation is acute. Something or someone you desire exacts a high price—but only if you give in. The chaotic Devil may manifest as others attempting to manipulate your better side; ask for a little angelic intervention, and resist.

Card Combinations

The cards placed around the Devil help reveal the nature of hidden energies around us. The second card can provide more information about the kind of temptation that the querent may be dealing with, and its impact.

THE DEVIL WITH THE ACE OF PENTACLES REVERSED
The temptation of money; a high price for security

THE DEVIL WITH THE TEN OF WANDS
A moral dilemma or obligation that brings a burden of guilt

XVI
THE TOWER

THE HOUSE OF GOD

The Tower means unavoidable disaster: literally, an act of God as implied by the card's alternative title, the House of God or *La Maison Dieu*. Like the arrow of love from Cupid or the scythe of Death, lightning can strike at any time. However, with ultimate destruction a new path is cleared for regeneration. In Greek myth, a flash of lightning emitted by Zeus impregnated Semele with her son Dionysus. Dionysus was the god of wine, and he is therefore associated with altered states—the aftershock that the Tower represents.

SYMBOLISM

The Tower can be seen as the Tower of Babel destroyed by God; the lightning striking the Tower represents divine retribution, and the fire symbolizes purification, which sparks a new beginning. In the Visconti-Sforza deck (above), intense rays of the sun appear to inflame the tower, and a cross falls with the two male figures. The cross symbolizes resurrection: the figures appear temporarily immobilized rather than dead, as if waiting to be reanimated. The falling figures on contemporary Tarots represent the fallout—emotional, physical, and spiritual—that comes with disaster. The card is numbered XVI, for the cosmic power of the elements.

ASTROLOGY

The Tower is associated with Mars, the fiery planet of war. Mars expresses the violent destruction and aftermath of release that the Tower may bring.

The Buddha and the Thunderbolt

In Buddhism, one of the sacred devotional objects is the *djore* (Tibet) or *vajra* (India), which means "thunderbolt." It represents the destruction of ignorance and the purification of the mind that is vital if one is to remove the imprint of the negative karma that we inherit at birth. The buddha of purification is Vajrasattva, a tantric deity who holds a *vajra* (or thunderbolt) in his right hand and a *ghanta* (or bell) for wisdom in the other. In Tantric ritual, the thunderbolt and bell are used together, so that their interaction signifies enlightenment. The *vajra* is also a symbol of the Hindu god Indra, king of heaven and god of rain, implying that a bolt of apparent destruction lights up the sky and the consciousness, so that purification—symbolized by water—can follow.

Upright Meaning: Disaster

The Tower represents sudden collapse. A bolt from the blue destroys what you have constructed: a lifestyle, business venture, relationship, or dream. Although the Tower signifies a fall, it does not suggest blame—only bad fortune that is unavoidable. In the aftermath, you can pick up the pieces and reclaim your ground. What you create now will have stronger foundations. Additional meanings include shock, and a breakthrough that illuminates the way ahead.

Reversed Meaning: Blame

The Tower reversed reveals disaster that may have been avoided. You may have created a basis for instability in your life, and now what you feared most has happened: the collapse of your dreams and an attack on your security. The upright Tower represents the sudden impact of Fate, yet you continue to suffer. Accept what has happened and forgive. Surrendering will help you rebuild your confidence and move forward.

Card Combinations

With the Star, a creative breakthrough; healing.
With the Three of Swords, a relationship truth.

XVII
THE STAR

The appearance of the Star is a call from the cosmos, offering divine inspiration, hope, creativity, and healing. The card may be depicted simply as a lone female figure gazing up at a guiding star; or, as in many contemporary decks, a maiden holding two cups, kneeling to pour her water into a pool and onto the earth.

SYMBOLISM

The star maiden of the Visconti-Sforza Tarot (above) reaches to touch a golden star, a powerful symbol of hope. We do not know her circumstances, but her stockinged feet are curious, given her elaborate dress and cloak. Her lack of shoes may denote vulnerability or poverty: things may not be as they seem at first glance. Later Tarots, as described above, show a maiden pouring water. This can signify the harmonious balance of nature, the flow of consciousness, and even the past (the earth) flowing into the present (the pool). The Star's number of XVII becomes eight (seven plus one), the number of points on the Visconti-Sforza card's star. Eight is the number of renewal, one of the symbolic meanings of water.

ASTROLOGY

The Star card is associated with Aquarius, the Water-carrier of the zodiac, associated with inspiration, ideas, and progress.

UPRIGHT MEANING: INSPIRATION

The Star reveals healing and harmony that are both physical and spiritual. Inner desires, which take form through your dreams,

can now be consciously expressed. This card is therefore fortuitous for artists and for entrepreneurs, but for everyone it is a sign of hope, energy, and boundless creativity. An additional meaning is spiritual or intuitive guidance.

REVERSED MEANING: CREATIVE BLOCK

The Star reversed can reveal a creative block, as with the reversed Magician (see page 69). You may not be able to fulfill your dreams just now; as starlight is bewitching, so is an impossible fantasy. In this context, the practical details that make a project hold true are overlooked. While it is compelling to dream, be aware that you need to identify your real-life expectations. This applies too to a dreamer in your life, who may lull you into partaking in a venture that has little chance of success.

CARD COMBINATIONS

A helpful reminder of the meaning of the Star in a reading is its star quality—it can show a major dream or need. The surrounding cards may reveal whether this dream complements or clashes with other major or minor events.

THE STAR WITH THE FIVE
OF PENTACLES (right)
A lack of resources; fear that
a dream will fail

 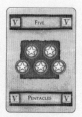

THE STAR WITH THE DEVIL (left)
A conflict between freedom and
restraint; a test

XVIII
THE MOON

The Moon reveals a crisis of faith. As moonlight makes the world look different—surreal, even—this card depicts the landscapes of the inner world or subconscious mind. Old or unresolved fears surface; the dark or hidden aspects of our personality, like night wolves, come out to play. In the shadows, we experience the dark night of the soul before we meet the Sun, the next card in the major arcana cycle.

SYMBOLISM

On the Visconti-Sforza card (right), a woman holds a crescent moon and bow. The moon is waning, toward the end of its cycle; the bow is broken, a symbol of failure. The female figure may represent the huntress Diana, who cannot pursue her quarry. In modern decks, two canines howl by two towers. The Twos symbolize tension and, here, a conflict of choice. With his body, the crayfish bridges a critical void between the unconscious and conscious mind. The water represents the inner emotions and the past; the dry land signifies the world beyond, which he must negotiate. The wolves symbolize instinct that cries for freedom. They are also fierce guardians, so the crayfish's journey—if he takes it—may involve a hazardous rite of passage. The crayfish represents the soul, and therefore our deepest yearnings. The Moon is numbered XVIII, which reduces to nine: eight plus one. In the minor arcana, Nines represent the ultimate expression of their suits (see page 137). Here, nine is the ultimate confusion of moonlight.

ASTROLOGY

The Moon's astrological sign is Pisces, the Fish. The association of the Fish with the soul and the element of water in which he dwells—representing the emotions—indicates the intensity of feeling linked with the Moon card.

102

UPRIGHT MEANING: DISILLUSION

The Moon shows disillusionment on the surface, but what lies beneath is a greater emotional turmoil. You may need to make a decision, but you cannot trust what you see; you may be feeling frustrated, confused, or fearful. It is important to rely on your instinct, as this is a time to follow your own innate wisdom. Additional meanings of the card include mysticism, intuitive knowing, and heeding the messages in dreams.

REVERSED MEANING: AVOIDANCE

In the reversed position, the Moon reveals the danger of doing nothing. While this brings temporary respite, it cannot bring you resolution. In order to avoid a decision, you may be tempted to seek refuge in the past, or find you are revising your expectation to fit what you think is on offer. The reversed Moon in readings can also reveal deception—by the self, or others.

CARD COMBINATIONS

Helpful keywords when interpreting the Moon are illusion, disillusion, and confusion. This is an emotional card, so any card that follows the Moon in a reading can indicate how the querent deals with their emotions and moves forward.

THE MOON WITH THE WORLD
Hesitation before the ending
of a phase; a need to let go of
the past

THE MOON WITH THE SUN
Success after soul-searching;
a release from uncertainty

XIX
THE SUN

Like the two preceding cosmic cards, the Moon and the Star, the Sun holds powerful energy: here, this is joy, success, and rejuvenation. The depiction of a sun and child or children on early and contemporary Tarots instantly communicates a radiant optimism. The Sun's life-giving warmth initiates renewal and growth; after the dark night of the Moon (see page 102) and the guidance of the Star (see page 100), we see the light. We arrive at an ideal destination, an earthly paradise in which we find protection and freedom.

SYMBOLISM

The Visconti-Sforza card (left) depicts a winged youth holding a sun with a human face. The sun represents the element of Fire; the cloud represents Air and Water, and the green plain, Earth. Later Tarots add a walled garden and sunflowers in bloom, which denote growth and energy. The garden wall is a metaphor for protection, security, and personal boundaries, while the huge sun signifies the self and the conscious mind. An Estensi Sun card shows a woman holding a spindle. This may be a reference to one of the Fates, Nona (the Greek Clotho), who spun the thread of human life. The Sun's number, XIX, stands for achievement, and also symbolizes the children and sun on Marseilles-style cards (see opposite): two children, each represented by X, with I denoting the sun.

ASTROLOGY

The Sun's astrological association is with the Sun, ruler of Leo, the sign concerned with confidence and the ego.

UPRIGHT MEANING: SUCCESS

The Sun is always a welcome card in a reading: its heat permeates all aspects of your life, bringing love, children, energy, happiness, and success. This is a card of rewards, bringing whatever you value; so you may enjoy a vacation, receive money, or find your creative muse. In terms of relationships and family, this is also a time to take sanctuary in love, and overall to experience the joy of all that you have achieved.

REVERSED MEANING: DELAY

The Sun reversed shows that heat and light, the gifts of the upright Sun, are just out of reach. You can envisage a carefree existence without worries about health, children, and work; this may take the form of a holiday in the sun, or simply a time when you can expend energy on enjoying your relationships rather than solving problems. It is important to keep the faith rather than give up, as this card indicates delay, not defeat.

CARD COMBINATIONS

Two keywords for the Sun are success and happiness. The cards that appear close to the Sun in a reading can show how a positive, productive phase is manifesting—in terms of relationships, finances, creativity, or simply recuperation.

THE SUN WITH THE ACE OF WANDS
A venture that attracts practical support; ideas and conversations inspire creativity and new projects

THE SUN WITH THE EMPRESS
A happy phase for a family in which success is shared; a new baby, a time of togetherness

XX Judgement

The Angel, The Trumpet, Fame

As the penultimate card in the major arcana cycle, Judgement reveals the need for self-assessment before reaching card XXI, the World—which is concerned with completion and rebirth—and a return to card 0, the Fool. Judgement is a part of the renewal process, where we come to terms with the past before moving on. This card is a call to examine our previous actions. Rather than await the decree of others, as in card VIII, Justice, here a question is posed: how do we judge ourselves?

Symbolism

The sword brandished by the authority figure on the Visconti-Sforza card (right) echoes the sword held by Justice (see page 82). Here, it has a similar purpose in that it represents time to evaluate the past. The angels blow bannered trumpets: this is a wake-up call, a time to be counted by one's conscience rather than by the external world. Modern decks such as *The Magic of Tarot* (see opposite) often show water as part of the card imagery. This signifies *aqua libra*, the water of life that brings purification and regeneration. The water also symbolizes the subconscious, again reinforcing the play of conscience when assessing past actions and behavior. On the Visconti-Sforza card, three figures look upward from a tomb. The two children mirror the angels, and the old man the heavenly figure above him. These are the earthly and spiritual sides of humans, indicating spiritual rebirth. The card is numbered XX, which reduces to two. This shows that we are close to integrating our conscious and unconscious selves; we are near to attaining the whole world.

Astrology

Judgement is associated with the planet Pluto. Pluto is concerned with identity and a quest for truth. Pluto was the Roman god of the underworld (the Hades of Greek myth). He expresses the need to examine the darker side of our natures, the message of Judgement, before moving forward.

ACCLAIMING TRUMPETS

In Jewish tradition, the shofar or trumpet is sounded to herald the beginning of a ten-day period, Rosh Hashanah, or "Feast of Trumpets," which ends with the Day of Atonement (Yom Kippur). The call of the shofar is a call to examine past behavior and recommit to the authority of God: "Awake, ye sleepers from your sleep...and ponder your deeds" (Numbers 29:1). For Latter Day Saints, seven trumpets will herald the end of the age with the Second Coming of Christ, when believers will be transformed into spirit.

The blowing of the trumpet or horn is also associated with the onset of battle. Those who died in battle in ancient times hoped their names would live on as a legacy for future generations, to achieve eponymous fame—an alternative title for Judgement. In this way, we might interpret the card in terms of deeds for which we would prefer to be remembered.

UPRIGHT MEANING: RENEWAL

An opportunity for renewal; a time of beginnings and endings during which you gain perspective on the past in order to move on. Judgement can bring self-acceptance and reward, rather than regret; you may look back, but with pleasure. This card can also indicate second chances, to take a fresh look at an old relationship, or to revisit an existing opportunity. Whatever your situation, events will move quickly, as this card indicates a faster pace.

REVERSED MEANING: GUILT

With Judgement in the reversed position, the chance to conclude a matter is delayed because you cannot confront fear of change. This card can indicate guilt, and therefore soul-searching holds you back. However, this can become so absorbing that you fail to notice what is going on in the present; opportunities may be missed if you cannot make peace with the past. Pay attention to your immediate needs, and take care of your physical body too.

CARD COMBINATIONS

With the High Priestess, a situation is assessed privately rather than spoken aloud.
With the Devil, it may be hard to move on and feel free in the world; you may need to forgive yourself for past actions.

XXI The World

The Universe

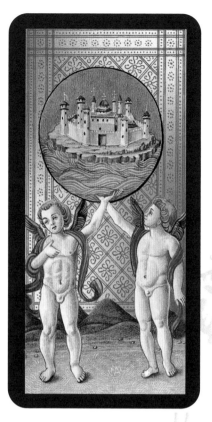

The World, or Universe—the final card in the twenty-two-card sequence of the major arcana—represents successful completion. Along with the Sun, it is one of the most positive cards in a reading. It brings the respect and acknowledgment of those who have witnessed your efforts.

Symbolism

In the Visconti-Sforza deck (left), two cherubs hold a globe depicting an island city under a starry sky. This symbolizes a heavenly paradise, a perfect world; the globe also signifies containment and completion. In the Marseilles and Rider Waite Smith decks, the garland forms the almond shape of a mandorla, which is used in religious iconography to frame holy figures. The mandorla symbolizes heaven on Earth. It is also the cosmic egg, a universal symbol of creation that implies the triumph of order over chaos. The card is numbered XXI: two plus one gives three, the number of creation. The figure on these cards appears to be both male and female. This intersex quality indicates the final integration of the unconscious and conscious, and the harmonious balance between humans and the greater universe.

Astrology

The World is associated with the planet Saturn, the astrological taskmaster. Saturn is concerned with objectivity and duty, and working within recognized boundaries. The World card shows that you have completed your work in a way that others can recognize and reward.

UPRIGHT MEANING: COMPLETION

The upright World card reveals success and a special reward. One part of your life is reaching a natural conclusion, and you are primed with energy and optimism about the future. It is time to take an essential step into the wider world. This can be expressed through the opportunity to explore literally by traveling, or by embarking on a new direction in your profession or a creative venture. Your lifestyle can change, as from now on you move on to even greater success and enjoy a way of being that embraces all that you desire. Completion and reward also bring opportunities for togetherness and celebrations.

REVERSED MEANING: DILUTION

The card in this position shows outdated values, or a situation that is unresolved or incomplete. Consequently, you are moving in ever-decreasing circles. As with Judgement reversed, you may miss out on immediate offers because you are unable to direct your energies to the present moment. This may be due to painful past issues, but there comes a time to pull away from familiar patterns.

CARD COMBINATIONS

When interpreting the World, consider that the card contains both beginnings and endings: in a reading, it can show that a new phase is already starting, so the cards that follow may reveal how you will proceed and what your journey will bring.

THE WORLD WITH THE FOOL (right)
The start of an inspiring and
successful phase that brings
excitement and travel

THE WORLD WITH JUSTICE (left)
A decision in your favor brings
satisfaction and closure

THE MINOR ARCANA

THE MINOR ARCANA COMPRISES fifty-six numbered cards that fall into four suits: Cups, Pentacles (Disks, Coins), Wands (Staves, Batons), and Swords. Each suit has ten numbered, or "pip" cards, from the Ace through Ten, and four people, or Court, cards: Page, Knight, Queen, and King. Historically, the minor arcana pips bore repeat suit symbols to denote their number: two Swords, Three Cups, or ten Pentacles, for example.

For the novice reader, there was little evocative imagery with which to play detective; if you were unfamiliar with the esoteric meaning of numbers or elements associated with the suits, there was little to guide you.

This changed in 1909 with the publication of the Rider Waite Smith deck, which illuminated the esoteric meanings of the minor arcana with fully illustrated pip cards. The artist was Pamela Colman Smith (1878–1951), directed by A. E. Waite (see page 18). It is likely that Colman Smith was influenced by a late-fifteenth century deck, the Sola Busca, the only known deck to have illustrated minor arcana cards prior to 1909 (and which was not commercially available until 1998). The Sola Busca was exhibited at the British Museum two years before the Rider deck appeared, hence the suggestion of influence; and two cards, the Three of Swords and Ten of Wands, bear a heavy compositional resemblance to those of the Sola Busca.

ABOVE: *The Five of Pentacles (Coins) of the Rider Waite Smith deck illustrates its literal meaning: feeling impoverished, excluded from comfort, and out in the cold.*

INTERPRETING THE MINOR ARCANA

The numbered, or pip, cards of the minor arcana are grouped together in this chapter, followed by sets of Pages, Knights, Queens, and Kings. The introductions to each set of cards offers guidance on the card's number or type and element.

ABOVE: *The Ace of Cups from the* Tarot of Marseilles. *The ornate chalice has eight sides like a baptismal font, symbolizing the idea of renewal and regeneration.*

INTERPRETING THE COURT CARDS

If you are a beginner, you may find the Court cards challenging, because they can refer to individuals. Physical attributes were once assigned to the Court cards, too—these are rarely used today, given the traditional descriptions do not encompass people of all ethnicities. As you read you may get an intuitive flash, identifying a Court card as an individual you know; but in general, it can be more helpful to look at the Courts in terms of personality types that also translate as an active influence. For example, if you were reading the Queen of Cups, this might traditionally indicate a sensitive, loving woman. If this is not manifesting in your life as a person, then the card means that these qualities are important to you—you may be acting as this Queen, or the card is advising you to apply her qualities of love and compassion to your situation. The Court cards can be read regardless of gender: a King, for example, can apply to a man or woman.

	UPRIGHT	REVERSED
CUPS:	Sensitive, kind, intuitive, imaginative	Uncommitted, overly idealistic
WANDS:	Passionate, motivated, communicative	Ego-driven, controlling
SWORDS:	Wise, direct, detached, instinctive	Ruthless, aggressive
PENTACLES:	Pragmatic, sensual, stable, generous	Untruthworthy, materialistic

INTERPRETING CARD PATTERNS

When reading the minor arcana, look at the pattern of cards before you in your spread. Assess the frequency of a suit: a spread laden with Pentacles, for example, would indicate material concerns: money, security, and property. A prevalence of Cups indicates that relationships and emotions dominate.

Some specific meanings have been attributed to the frequency of cards of the same number and type in a reading. A. E. Waite, creator of the Rider Waite Smith deck (see page 18), includes a list of meanings in his book *The Pictorial Key to the Tarot*. The list overleaf has been adapted from his original.

Upright

FOUR KINGS: Acknowledgment, acclaim
THREE KINGS: Consultation, advice
TWO KINGS: Minor counsel

FOUR QUEENS: Great debate
THREE QUEENS: Deception
TWO QUEENS: Sincere friendship

FOUR KNIGHTS: Serious matters
THREE KNIGHTS: Lively discussion
TWO KNIGHTS: Intimacy

FOUR PAGES: Potential illness
THREE PAGES: Dispute
TWO PAGES: Disquiet

FOUR TENS: Criticism
THREE TENS: A new situation
TWO TENS: Change

FOUR NINES: A good friend
THREE NINES: Success
TWO NINES: Acceptance

FOUR EIGHTS: A reversal
THREE EIGHTS: Marriage
TWO EIGHTS: New knowledge

FOUR SEVENS: Intrigue
THREE SEVENS: Vulnerability
TWO SEVENS: News

FOUR SIXES: Abundance, advantages
THREE SIXES: Success
TWO SIXES: Irritability

FOUR FIVES: Regularity, balance
THREE FIVES: Determination
TWO FIVES: Delay, awaiting a result

FOUR FOURS: A journey
THREE FOURS: Reflection
TWO FOURS: Insomnia

FOUR THREES: Progress
THREE THREES: Unity
TWO THREES: Calm

FOUR TWOS: Contention, conflict
THREE TWOS: Security
TWO TWOS: Accord, balance

FOUR ACES: Favorable opportunities
THREE ACES: A small triumph, good news
TWO ACES: Trickery

Reversed

FOUR KINGS: Swift movement
THREE KINGS: Commerce
TWO KINGS: Projects

FOUR QUEENS: Bad company
THREE QUEENS: Overindulgence
TWO QUEENS: Work

FOUR KNIGHTS: Alliance
THREE KNIGHTS: An encounter
TWO KNIGHTS: Susceptibility

FOUR PAGES: Hardship
THREE PAGES: Idleness
TWO PAGES: Society

FOUR TENS: Current event
THREE TENS: Disappointment
TWO TENS: Justified expectation

FOUR NINES: Exploitation
THREE NINES: Carelessness
TWO NINES: A small profit

FOUR EIGHTS: Error
THREE EIGHTS: A spectacle
TWO EIGHTS: Misfortune

FOUR SEVENS: Quarrelers
THREE SEVENS: Joy
TWO SEVENS: Faithlessness

FOUR SIXES: Care
THREE SIXES: Satisfaction
TWO SIXES: Failure

FOUR FIVES: Order
THREE FIVES: Hesitation
TWO FIVES: Reverse

FOUR FOURS: Walks abroad; attention
THREE FOURS: Disquiet
TWO FOURS: Dispute

FOUR THREES: Great success
THREE THREES: Serenity
TWO THREES: Safety

FOUR TWOS: Reconciliation
THREE TWOS: Apprehension
TWO TWOS: Mistrust

FOUR ACES: Dishonor
THREE ACES: Excess
TWO ACES: Enemies

THE ACES

THE ACES of the minor arcana reveal new themes in life. They can be seen as the primal essences of their suits, denoting action, beginnings, and opportunities. Consider the meaning of the suits in terms of their associated elements (see page 21). For example, the suit of Swords is associated with the element of Air—so mental activity, action, and conflict are its values. The Ace of Swords, being the root of the suit, reveals victory and action.

The Aces can be seen as gifts—in the Rider Waite Smith Aces, each suit icon is handed to the reader (see background image, right, where the cup sits in an outstretched hand). As the gift of the Aces is offered to you, so you need to receive its energy, and take action to maximize its potential.

113

ACE OF CUPS

UPRIGHT MEANING

The suit of Cups is associated with the element of Water, the symbol of flowing emotions. The Ace ushers in a period when emotions and relationships are foremost, and can reveal pregnancy and motherhood. It signifies a phase in which feelings are expressed and reciprocated, and can predict one important love partnership. This is also an auspicious card for creative activities, when original projects get started and inspiration comes naturally.

REVERSED MEANING

When reversed, the Ace shows emotions suppressed or out of control, so unhappiness or fears about a relationship may cause concern. There may be worries about children and family, and a lack of understanding between parents or siblings. This is a common card for those struggling to balance home and work. Bear in mind that the Ace in this position often reflects insecurity or fear about the future, not reality. Just as the cup can suddenly overturn, so it can right itself.

ACE OF PENTACLES

UPRIGHT MEANING

The suit of Pentacles takes the element of Earth, so the Ace of Pentacles brings the energy of money and opportunities to make it. As Aces denote beginnings, the card can reveal new ways to create the reality you desire, to establish something that has value for you. Money may come in the form of a pay rise, investments, savings schemes, and even spontaneous gambles. The card relates to property matters, too, so finding a home or remodeling your existing home are additional interpretations.

REVERSED MEANING

Imbalance in financial affairs. The Ace reversed can reveal an obsession with money that masks a lack, or neglect, of other responsibilities, so priorities are skewed. This is a fruitless pursuit; pinning all your hopes on one outcome alone diverts you from finding the real treasures—the genuine projects and people who can inspire you. This card may reveal the influences of greed around you, so beware of an acquisitive streak.

ACE OF WANDS

UPRIGHT MEANING

The suit of Wands represents negotiation and creativity. The Ace of Wands is pure fiery masculine energy—as shown by the phallic nature of the wand. The card reveals the blossoming of new ventures, favoring travel, beginning a new career, or starting a family. It is now time to use your ability to communicate with others to great effectiveness.

REVERSED MEANING

In the reversed position, the Ace of Wands can indicate problems with masculinity and creativity—in a reading, it can reveal a relationship in which a lover lacks commitment, or where one partner must wait for the other. In general, the Ace reversed reveals a degree of separation or delay that blocks results. Partnerships, business dealings, or travel plans may therefore suffer from a lack of organization, poor timing, or miscommunication.

ACE OF SWORDS

UPRIGHT MEANING

The suit of Swords relates to the element of Air, which is associated with the realm of the intellect. When this card appears in a reading, it shows that your mental agility will bring you success. The Ace also predicts a time of challenge and possible conflict that forces you into action. As this is an innovative card, it foretells mindful energy that will fuel new projects and help you deal assertively with others.

REVERSED MEANING

In the reversed position, the Ace of Swords reveals that you are being held back in some way, which leads to frustration and delay. It can indicate a failure of will, lack of confidence in your intellectual abilities, or opposition that undermines your power. As all Sword cards call upon your innermost resources, believe that you have the strength of character to withstand the situation.

THE TWOS

TWOS STAND FOR balance, partnerships, and the flow of energy between opposite or compatible forces. The Two cards can show a pending decision or harmonious alignment, depending on their particular suit. With Wands, for example, the suit of negotiation and creativity, the Two reveals progress; with the martial Swords (shown left), the Two suggests procrastination or a truce, while the Two of Pentacles denotes choices.

TWO OF CUPS

UPRIGHT MEANING

The upright Two predicts natural harmony between two people. It reveals happy agreements and love, so a relationship may be sealed by an engagement or marriage. Two also sees friendships flourish as you instinctively know how to support and laugh with those around you. Creative partnerships are the message here too, so appreciate those significant others. A writing partner, colleague, or someone with whom you are studying brings you inspiration.

REVERSED MEANING

As the upright Two shows affinity, the Two reversed indicates secrets and possibly betrayal. If you are considering a commitment to a partner, it is better to delay your decision until you can really talk with one another. This is a testing time for all relationships when you may not feel you can trust those you usually rely upon. It is best to keep your doubts to yourself just now, and trust only your own judgement.

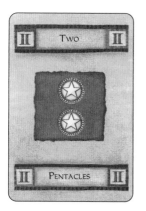

TWO OF PENTACLES

UPRIGHT MEANING

This Two represents balance and cashflow—as money comes in and goes out, you may need to prioritize certain payments. This Two also predicts financial solvency and productive business partnerships. In broader terms, this is the card of choices, showing a decision about, for example, a location, study, or work.

REVERSED MEANING

A partnership suffers when the Two is reversed. Rather than have cooperation, one of you puts in more effort than the other, leading to financial loss. The Two can reveal an unworkable liaison—a colleague or manager may not deliver what they claim. Viewed as an indication of a situation rather than an individual, a new venture may not take off due to lack of funding, which leads to worry and frustration. Take this card as a warning to examine the motives of those whom you choose to trust.

Two of Wands

Upright Meaning

You are moving forward; those who have influence are listening to what you have to say. This card represents ideas and planning, and seeing opportunities that will lead to future success and stability. The Two also denotes trust and partnerships that bring reward, particularly in terms of expanding an existing business or taking a step up in your career. You will receive support and interest from others to ensure steady progress.

Reversed Meaning

In the reversed position, the Two can warn you that your talent may be wasted while others look on. If you value what you do, look elsewhere for likeminded individuals who appreciate your ingenuity. The Two reversed can predict misplaced trust in an unreliable partner: a lover, friend, or work associate. This, as in all the reversed Twos, is the imbalance to watch out for. Expect others to meet you halfway.

Two of Swords

Upright Meaning

The Two of Swords can be taken literally, as someone you cross swords with in potential conflict. However, it is also a resting position before and after a battle of wits, and, in this sense, the Two reveals a truce or a stalemate; more generally, the card shows procrastination. While this may appear to be a welcome respite, you will need to face an issue eventually. When this thinking time expires, draw on your courage, rely on your intellect, and make your decision.

Reversed Meaning

The Two reversed reveals a deception, often concerning a partnership. The stalemate of the upright card goes deeper here, as an opponent uses his or her time to manipulate the truth. When this card appears in a reading, it is best not to accept someone else's findings; thoroughly investigate a situation for yourself. It is worth fighting through a web of misdirection to get to the heart of an important matter.

THE THREES

ONE, TWO, THREE: GO. Three is the point at which everything begins, from blowing out candles on a cake to running a race. Three is the number of creation and life (see page 36), the dynamic synthesis of primal one and balanced two.

As with the other number cards, the suit elements define how the Threes are expressed. In the fiery suit of Wands, the Three sees the development of an idea into reality; the feudal Three of Swords, with its element of Air for decisions and conflict, can foretell heartbreak.

THREE OF CUPS

UPRIGHT MEANING

This is a card of great happiness and a renewed belief in love. Your relationships and those of the people around you develop, so the atmosphere is joyful. Given the harmony of this card, it also brings healing and recovery to those who have felt at a low ebb. It reveals new energy and life, and can also foretell a new baby—literally, or in the form of a precious project. Your social life benefits from parties and get-togethers, and you enjoy life's pleasures. An additional meaning is flirtation and indulgence.

REVERSED MEANING

This reversed Three brings distance and discord. Disappointment or emotional betrayal creates a barrier in partnerships. The happiness in the upright card is dissipated, so there may be disappointment and disbelief. The Three can also reveal irritating health problems, which in turn are often the result of dissatisfaction or discomfort in emotional matters.

THREE OF PENTACLES

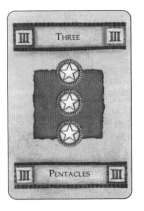

UPRIGHT MEANING

You can now do what you do best. The Three of Pentacles is the symbol of the craftsperson, who begins with one idea and from it produces something of value. This is a time of tangible, early success, when hard work and application bring reward in terms of finances, but also creative satisfaction. You can feel pleased with your achievement because it is the result of your personal effort and vision.

REVERSED MEANING

There is an element of a project—or life in general—that you cannot face just now: the work itself. You want to have the fruits of your labor without the labor, or perhaps an ideal is blinding you to the reality. Consider that poor planning or rushing to complete the least interesting aspects of a job may be at the root of this. Begin again and recommit to the boring detail to get what you want in the long term, or abandon this avenue rather than crave distraction.

THREE OF WANDS

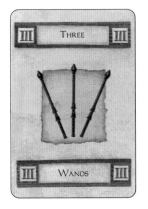

UPRIGHT MEANING

This is a time of personal gain and reward when you let others see what motivates you through your work. The Three presents an inspired opportunity for self-expression through art, music, dance, and crafts. Through this, you can assert your individuality, so nurture your quirks and love your eccentricities. An additional meaning is travel and overall, a broadening of your horizons.

REVERSED MEANING

The Three reversed tells of a breakdown in communication. This card shows an inability to express your ideas, along with frustrating delays to projects and plans. This situation creates tension around you as it is hard to garner support. In this situation, it may be best to slow your pace—declutter your thinking and simplify your plans until this influence shifts.

THREE OF SWORDS

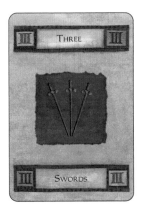

UPRIGHT MEANING

The Three of Swords reveals tears, loss, and heartbreak. The three swords can show three people in a relationship, so the card also suggests affairs and betrayal. Alternatively, another dream you held close to your heart is no longer feasible. The one solace is that the meaning of the Three is not ambiguous, so when it falls in a future position in a reading it can at least act as a warning that truth is coming. This may cause you pain, but it is the only way to get to the happier relationships that await.

REVERSED MEANING

In the reversed position, heartbreak is accompanied by quarreling and general disorder. Although this sounds negative, expressing the upheaval can at least release and relieve the tension. This is a tumultuous time, and it can be experienced as anxiety rather than an external drama. Bear in mind that this is a minor arcana card, and its influence will pass.

THE FOURS

FOURS ARE EVEN and stable. Four is the number of sides of a square, an ancient symbol for Earth in India and China. In Pythagorean theory, four was the first number to create a solid—the tetrahedron, or pyramid, with a base and three sides. Four relates to structure: the four-armed cross, the four principal compass points, the four elements, and to the organization of the Tarot itself. There are four suits in the deck and four Court cards per suit, leaving forty numbered or "pip" cards.

In a reading, the Fours reveal practical situations rather than esoteric matters. They indicate stability or rigidity, depending again on the qualities of the particular suit. In the emotional suit of Cups, they reveal inaction or boredom, whereas in the suit of Swords, the lack of activity represents a welcome rest from conflict.

FOUR OF CUPS

UPRIGHT MEANING

The Four of Cups shows a stuck situation or relationship. This may be temporary, but for the partnership to grow you need to revaluate what brought you together and go forward as one or both of you may be feeling restless or mildly bored. More generally, nothing is seriously amiss as you continue from day to day, but that feeling of flatness may be a sign that you need change—to find energy, and inspiration.

REVERSED MEANING

In the reversed position, the Four indicates instability and deadlock; this may drain your energy and leave you feeling low. Equally, this influence could see you submerge yourself in work or other time-hungry activities to avoid confronting a suffocating situation or relationship. The action you need to take to resolve matters may seem daunting, but you can regain your equilibrium.

FOUR OF PENTACLES

UPRIGHT MEANING

Financial security is the message of the upright Four. You may have suffered hardship and have had to work too hard and for too long, and now your input pays off, bringing satisfaction and reward. You find relief and can ease off a little, mindful that you have everything you need. As the pressure eases and you relax, health matters also improve. This card comes with a caution, however, against materialism.

REVERSED MEANING

The Four reversed shows struggle. This may be because you cannot believe that money may come easily to you and that you are deserving of it. This lack of confidence may not give others the right signals about you, and consequently opportunities are missed. This card can also reveal challenging departmental structures at work, internal politics, and poor financial management.

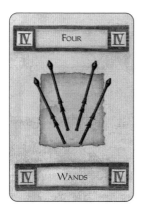

Four of Wands

Upright Meaning

This Four suggests a great social life and happiness. As the Wands bud with ideas, you may be inspired to move to a new home, extend your existing dwelling, or simply spend time in a place you love. Workwise, others show their appreciation of your originality. You are part of every conversation and feel wanted and involved. Additional meanings of the card include vacations and honeymoons.

Reversed Meaning

The Four reversed reveals the restrictive meaning of the Fours: narrow attitudes block your route to success and may make you feel invisible. As others actively progress and are praised, you feel you don't fit in; this could be your inflexibility, or theirs. Whatever the case, examine your values and those of others carefully, then decide what or whom needs to change.

Four of Swords

Upright Meaning

The Four in this difficult suit means neutrality; for once, nothing is happening: no conflict or strife, but equally, no passion. It denotes rest and recuperation—this may be physical illness from which you can now recover, or time out from a relationship or job. Whichever applies, it is likely that your energy levels are low, but this break may give you much-needed time to think.

Reversed Meaning

Whereas the upright Four is a welcome rest, the reversed Four imposes time away. This creates a sense of isolation and possibly resentment that blurs the benefits you may get from being away from home or work. It is better to surrender than fight another's decision, no matter how incomprehensible it may seem. Choose peace; you may feel overruled, but it's not forever.

THE FIVES

FIVE is the number of mankind. The five-pointed star is the template for the form of an outstretched human being, with the head, hands, and feet marking each segment. The star is also the emblem of the Hindu god Shiva, who both creates and destroys. This is the double aspect of five: the problems we encounter are manmade—we suffer for them, but can easily extricate ourselves. As we have five fingers, so we have a hand in our own destiny and design.

Unusually, Fives have a similar meaning in all the minor arcana suits. A Five reveals a test. In the suit of Cups this is a test of emotional strength; in Wands, of capability; in Pentacles, of resources; and in Swords, a test of will.

FIVE OF CUPS

UPRIGHT MEANING

The Five of Cups is the natural outcome of the restless Four. Because small problems in a relationship have been neglected in the past, deeper doubt has taken root. Feelings are no longer hidden and emotions run wild: disappointment, sadness, and regret. This card can often indicate a relationship breaking up, or at least a time of separation when you both take time out to revaluate your partnership. Additional meanings include a loss, such as bereavement.

REVERSED MEANING

The Five of Cups is one of the few minor arcana cards that has a positive meaning when reversed. This card reveals that you have reached the lowest point in a particular cycle; you have suffered, but are now in the healing process. After loss or rejection, you know that what remains is more hopeful. You see a glimmer of the future before you, and you are now stronger and ready to move on.

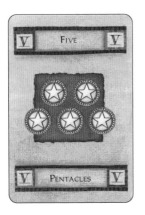

FIVE OF PENTACLES

UPRIGHT MEANING

The obvious meaning of this Five is being poor and feeling lost. It denotes financial difficulties, such as debt and its associated stress, but bear in mind that the Five often mirrors a fear of losing money, friendship, or love, rather than actual scarcity. When this card appears, it indicates that you are feeling cast out and marginalized because having money often means earning a place in society.

REVERSED MEANING

A poor decision leaves you feeling impoverished. This is a warning not to cling to possessions or money for their own sake, because what you want may desert you. This applies both to finances and to relationships, so equally you may be on the receiving end of a partner's selfishness, which ultimately endangers your partnership. Reconsider your priorities, as your values are under scrutiny.

FIVE OF WANDS

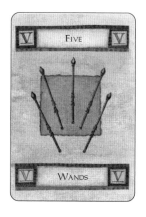

UPRIGHT MEANING

The Five of Wands shows challenges to your position, and you may feel you are not being listened to. The message here is to remain steadfast rather than step back and appease others. Regardless of how well you usually handle pressure, these tests may be quite different from those of the past. Attend to every detail—double-check travel plans, schedules, accounts, agendas, and appointments—and make sure everyone understands your intentions.

REVERSED MEANING

This Five carries the message of deception. You are hemmed in by another's dishonesty and there is little you can do to change the course of events, other than be clear that you are not to blame. As the Wands suit is concerned with negotiation and talking, it is likely that you will have heard words that lead you to conclude you have been dealing with an untruthful or unreliable person.

FIVE OF SWORDS

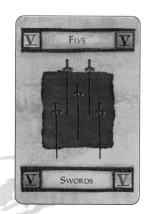

UPRIGHT MEANING

What exactly are you fighting for? This challenge can only deplete you, and you cannot win. It may be difficult to abandon the cause, but the Five of Swords indicates that it is time to walk away. The card traditionally shows oppression, humiliation, and, potentially, bullying. Now the outcome is clear, you can make plans elsewhere.

REVERSED MEANING

When the Five is in the reversed position, the upright meaning can be intensified. A further interpretation is that the conflict is not genuine—purely a show of strength or ego to cover up frailty or incompetence, which may be driven by fear. See the situation for what it is, and be willing to move on.

THE SIXES

AFTER THE TUMULTUOUS Fives, the Sixes denote harmony and passivity. Six forms the Star of David, which comprises one upright and one inverted triangle to represent the soul on Earth—an idea balanced by its expression. The Sixes often reveal two themes or ideas that work together productively, but there is also a sense of hesitation as we see the void between what we have and what is possible. In the book of Genesis, the world was created from chaos in six days, so there is a sense of evolution and history about Six.

Sixes and Fours can be difficult for new readers to differentiate, because they both appear inactive and stable. Imagine that Four signifies order and structure, whereas Six is its natural progression: contentment and balance. As with all minor arcana cards, the element of each suit modifies the meaning. In the emotional suit of Cups, Six reveals the past meeting the present; in the fiery Six of Wands, we see achievement and recognition.

SIX OF CUPS

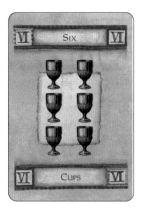

UPRIGHT MEANING

When the Six of Cups appears in your reading, memories resurface and you reminisce. Mentally, this may be a time when you flit in and out of two worlds: your nostalgic past and happy present. You may meet an old acquaintance who links you with a future project or relationship—this card is known as "the Visitor," reconnecting you with people from your past. In general, this is a time to appreciate what experience has taught you, and enjoy a new lease of life.

REVERSED MEANING

When the Six of Cups is reversed, a touch of nostalgia becomes sentimentality, along with a refusal to move on from the past. Inherent in this reverie is the idea that the past is a refuge, a convenient way to avoid present issues that are unsatisfactory. This may be expressed as clinginess toward others, or absorption in their needs to the exclusion of yours.

SIX OF PENTACLES

UPRIGHT MEANING

The upright Six of Pentacles shows that there is a beneficent understanding between you and those people who are close to you. During this happy phase you attract genuine help from above— for example, you may receive investment funding for a business from a mentor, a small cash sum, or an unexpected gift from a good friend. These boons, both great and small, show others' appreciation of you and their unstinting support. In return, you give unreservedly to them.

REVERSED MEANING

As the upright Six reveals support and abundance, so the reversed card indicates meanness of spirit and financial withdrawal. Money promised to you will not be forthcoming, or what you are offered is not honestly given or truly available. It is advisable not to accept what little is on offer; hold out for the full amount, or write off the debt rather than buy into a deal or situation that compromises your values.

Six of Wands

Upright Meaning

The upright Six of Wands brings success, deserved rewards, and recognition. This may be the favorable resolution of a legal matter, passing exams, or winning a promotion or new contract. There is a sense of triumph here, because now all your hard effort in the past feels truly worthwhile. However, this card comes with a small caution: examine carefully any offers in hand to ensure that all promises made will be fulfilled.

Reversed Meaning

The Six of Wands reversed foretells delays to plans and a fear about their outcome. However, this does not mean you suffer from outright failure—simply a truly frustrating wait, during which you try to discover the right outlet for your dreams. This card can also show that other people may have let you down recently; you may worry about what they are saying behind your back. This atmosphere of insecurity may cause you to feel hesitant.

Six of Swords

Upright Meaning

The upright Six brings peace of mind after trouble. You move away from stress, and may travel, for work or pleasure. This gives you a chance to breathe again and refuel your energy; it may even lead to a valuable discovery of some kind. Do not worry that this time represents closure or an ending—it is just a part of life's natural ebb and flow. Relax, and return with energy and enthusiasm.

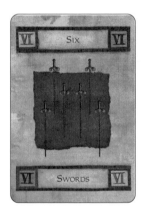

Reversed Meaning

The Six of Swords reversed can reveal a missed opportunity. As a result, the world shrinks rather than expands, and you feel in limbo. This card can also warn that you cannot rest just now; a retreat—the gift of this card in the upright position—may not be available just now. With effort, however, you can work through every problem in turn and gradually make progress.

THE SEVENS

SEVEN HAS A reputation as a mystical number. It was sacred to the god Apollo, the inspiration for the famous Delphic oracle; in classical wisdom it was believed that there were seven planets in the solar system: the Sun, the Moon, Mercury, Venus, Mars, Jupiter, and Saturn; and in Eastern healing there are seven *chakras*, or energy vortexes, in the human body. In folklore, the seventh son of a seventh son was thought to be blessed with magical healing ability.

Number theorists suggest that because it is a prime number, indivisible by any other, Seven represents unification. In the Tarot minor arcana, this reveals the bringing together of one's resources. It also represents potential because it is made up of three (the number for heaven) and four (for Earth), indicating the possibility of greatness through integration. In a reading, consider that all the Sevens share this theme of potential and the need for integrity and perception.

SEVEN OF CUPS

UPRIGHT MEANING

The Seven of Cups reveals that you may question a recent offer. You are following a dream, but make sure that this opportunity will deliver. Confusion and indecision abound with this card, so you have only your instinct to rely upon. To banish doubt, retrace your reactions and remember your first impression, rather than the reasoned arguments that may have followed. This is a time of great creativity; just ensure that whatever or whomever you are now dealing with is right for you.

REVERSED MEANING

The reversed Seven indicates the danger of idealizing a person or situation in order to avoid an unpalatable truth. You may be so keen to succeed, or your desires so overwhelming, that you delude yourself. An alternative meaning of this card is that you are deceived not by your own fantasies but by a lover. The message is not to take anything for granted.

SEVEN OF PENTACLES

UPRIGHT MEANING

The Seven of Pentacles tells you that you must keep on going, because there is more on offer. Work on a long-term project looks promising, but it is not time to rest yet—plans will come to fruition, but only with steady application and willpower. Believe that your goal is worthwhile, and visualize what you want by achieving it. This card often applies to tedious jobs, in your career, education, and home, for example, and its message is unrelenting, too: persevere.

REVERSED MEANING

Like the upright Seven of Pentacles, the reversed card also reveals the need to act. However, this is because progress is non-existent: time has been wasted, and money problems may be the result of doing too little too late—or nothing at all. Opportunities will dwindle and anxiety about finances will only fester, so it may be better to commit or quit.

SEVEN OF WANDS

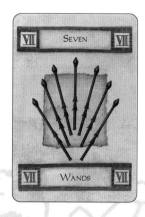

UPRIGHT MEANING

Just as the Seven of Pentacles urges action, so the Seven of Wands shows the need to keep talking, and stay true to your values, in spite of all the difficult debate or arguments around you. Think that you have six physical wands to your side, and that the seventh lies in your path; this seventh wand is your only obstacle, which can be overcome. Look at this barrier up close; it is only one more piece of debris, which will disappear if you stay true to your purpose.

REVERSED MEANING

In the reversed position, the Seven shows serious concerns about the work you are doing. A project or current contract may feel unworkable and without purpose, which in turn causes you to doubt your position. At this time, there are simply too many challenging issues to deflect or resolve. It is best to conserve your energy and do whatever is necessary to allay stress.

SEVEN OF SWORDS

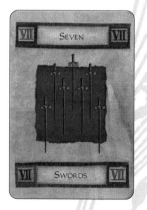

UPRIGHT MEANING

As the Sevens indicate the need for perception, the martial Seven of Swords calls for an expert plan to disarm an adversary. You may be feeling cornered, but your intellect may prove to be your best ally. You or someone in your orbit may resort to deviousness. The watchwords are protection and strategy, to safeguard what you value. A further meaning is to double-check home security and keep valuables close.

REVERSED MEANING

The Seven of Swords reversed can reveal that you give up on a fight too soon. Be adamant about what you want, and be prepared to make a forceful stand for it rather than give in to others' tactics.

THE EIGHTS

THE EIGHTS IN THE minor arcana signify change. This may appear inconsistent with the other even numbers—two, four, and six—which indicate stability, as the natural tension of opposites is balanced. However, as the numbered minor arcana suits run from the Aces (the gifts of the suits) to the completion of the Tens, the Eights hold the history of our experience. With this accumulation, decisions beckon.

Eight is associated with the Greek god Hermes because the number forms part of the shape of the magic wand, or caduceus, that he carried. Eight is also the lemniscate that appears on the Magician and Strength cards (see pages 68 and 88). Hermes was the gods' messenger, and he and his number are associated with movement and change. Although change can bring anxiety, its purpose is renewal. Baptismal fonts have eight sides as a symbol of regeneration.

The Eights also carry the theme of assessment and judgement. The Eight of Cups, for example, denotes a change of heart. The Eight of Wands reveals an adjustment to a faster pace of life, but also a time to reap reward.

EIGHT OF CUPS

UPRIGHT MEANING

The Eight of Cups indicates change. This may relate to a change of heart in a relationship or another situation that can progress no further. There may be no fault with the other party, but you turn away to seek what you need elsewhere. This is a decision you take to protect yourself in the long term.

REVERSED MEANING

As you might expect, the reversed Eight of Swords shows an error of judgement. You may walk away from an established relationship or other opportunity because you cannot appreciate its worth. Whereas the upright Eight of Cups reveals a mature decision, the reversed Eight is impulsive. Alternatively, you may be the victim of another's poor judgement when they abandon you in order to satisfy their ego elsewhere.

EIGHT OF PENTACLES

UPRIGHT MEANING

The Eight reveals money and reward for talent and skill. This brings a sense of liberation and the belief that doing what you love can support you financially. A further meaning is obtaining qualifications and success in examinations. Overall, this Eight stands for professionalism and perfectionism, and you hold yourself to high standards.

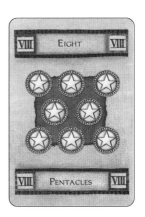

REVERSED MEANING

Restriction: being in the wrong place or position, that makes you doubt your ambition and direction. The Eight reversed can also show that you are motivated solely by money, possibly because a soul-destroying project or work has little else to offer.

EIGHT OF WANDS

UPRIGHT MEANING

The Eight of Wands brings news. This is a fast and frenetic time when communication is key and opportunities and offers come in. You may travel, partake in a creative collaboration, be inspired by talking to stimulating individuals, or contribute to a community project. If you are waiting for answers, this card tells you "yes."

REVERSED MEANING

In the reversed position, the Eight of Wands shows a degree of confusion because you cannot seem to connect with those you want to deal with, or be clear about what they want. When you try to communicate, you miss the mark: texts, messages, and emails disappear. All you can do is be patient. Avoid making important journeys or signing agreements just now.

EIGHT OF SWORDS

UPRIGHT MEANING

The Eight is the card of restriction. It can signify a setback and, more generally, a way of thinking. The effect is feeling blocked, but it is possible to think your way out of this, to give yourself permission to see what has held you back, admit mistakes, then take a new approach. In love relationships, the card can show that one partner is unavailable, physically and/or emotionally, so the relationship is restricted, hidden, or one-sided.

REVERSED MEANING

The Eight of Swords reversed reveals frustration, and in some cases outright despair and anger. You may feel furious with yourself and lash out at others because you need an outlet for your inability to accept a difficult situation. The way out is to drop your defences; telling the truth frees you to see a way out. Use your head, rather than lose it.

THE NINES

NINES ARE KNOWN AS the "ultimates" of their suits, where the intrinsic value of each suit finds maximum expression. Nine represents the triple triad of mind, body, and spirit; it also expresses order and spiritual integration. In Taoism, nine numbered squares complete the Lo Shu, the magical template that is used to calculate the effects of time and *chi* energy on a building. In this sense, the Nines express the idea of foundation.

With the Nines, it is helpful to recall the suit element meanings and develop them to their utmost. As Cups represent Water and the emotions, the Nine crowns you with wishes fulfilled, while Earth-bound Pentacles reveal a material gain. As ever, the troublesome Swords represent conflict—in Nine, an accumulation of thoughts, resulting in anxiety. However, as with all battles, there is always a way to move forward.

NINE OF CUPS

UPRIGHT MEANING

The Nine of Cups is often referred to as the "wish card" in a reading. It means that a dream may come true; everything you hope for can become reality. This abundant card shows a surfeit of affection and fun, and a perfect balance in all your relationships. This is a time for wonderful social opportunities, new friendships, and intimate partnerships. There is a natural flow about life now, and health matters are also favored.

REVERSED MEANING

In the reversed position, the Nine shows imbalance in the realm of the affections. This may manifest as self-absorption, when you neglect those closest to you, alienating friends and lovers in the process. Alternatively, you may feel sidelined by another person's obsession with me, me, me. As the upright card shows an easy connection with others, so the Nine reversed reveals delays or emotional disconnection.

NINE OF PENTACLES

UPRIGHT MEANING

The Nine of Pentacles shows a time for reward and luxuries. You have achieved material stability through hard work and financial acumen, and now you have time for leisure. For the organized, you can enjoy putting your house in order or tending the garden, and prizing your home. Small problems are resolved under this card's influence, and domestic peace abounds. Your natural contentment is attractive to others, so be prepared for a meeting of minds.

REVERSED MEANING

Your domestic sanctuary may be under siege when the Nine of Pentacles reverses. Irresponsibility with money, or an unwillingness to deal with debts or confront disputes, leaves you vulnerable to feelings of insecurity. To safeguard your home and heal the predicament, you need to take a more reasonable approach to problem-solving. Look at alternatives, as a resolution is possible.

NINE OF WANDS

UPRIGHT MEANING

You are in a strong position. However, the card asks you to be efficient, to use your energy and resources wisely in order to keep going. Protect yourself during this creative, demanding phase so you keep what you have worked for. In friendships and relationships, you may need to be discerning about whom you let in to your circle, although others can offer support and financial help. An additional meaning of the card is trust issues due to past hurt.

REVERSED MEANING

The Nine of Wands reversed reveals that you may be drowning under others' constant demands on your time, which are draining you. There is little satisfaction to be gained when you can only be concerned with completion rather than enjoying the journey. It is best not to give in to other people's pressure, although unfortunately this can become a way of life. Distance yourself and spend more time considering your own needs, rather than appeasing others.

NINE OF SWORDS

UPRIGHT MEANING

Whereas many of the Swords cards depict suffering in external situations, such as the heartbreak Three or harsh Five, the Nine is concerned with internal processes. It can mean stress and worry, which may take the form of anxiety about the future, worry about the self or others, nightmares, insomnia, or random, anxious thoughts. A stuck situation intensifies, and the mind is busy playing out every possible scenario. An additional meaning of the card is any physical pain or discomfort that disturbs sleep.

REVERSED MEANING

Unfortunately, the reversed Nine of Swords intensifies the experience of anxiety associated with the upright card. In this instance there may be feelings of despair and entrapment. However, you can get through this testing time. Ask for help and you can find a way to restore your faith.

THE TENS

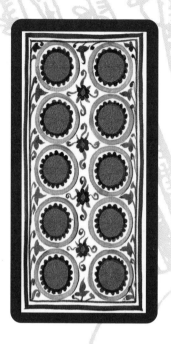

TENS STAND FOR completeness and perfection. Ten is also a mystic number with myriad examples of its importance—the Ten Commandments of the Old Testament; the astrological decan, or ten degrees of a zodiac sign, as a predictor of personality types; the ten spheres, or aspects of God, on the Tree of Life in Hebrew mysticism. The Nines are the ultimate expression of each suit, while the Tens present them as final outcomes. When the cycle is complete, it begins again, so the idea of Ten encompasses endings and beginnings.

In the minor arcana suits, the Ten's sheer number can reveal the greatest happiness or the heaviest burdens. The Ten of Wands reveals the weight of the world on your shoulders; in Cups, the love of family; in the suit of Swords, the focus moves from conflict to endings; and in Pentacles, the Ten represents the most that money and security can bring.

TEN OF CUPS

UPRIGHT MEANING

The Ten of Cups reveals complete contentment in relationships. It highlights the love of a family for one another, and this encompasses family in its broadest sense—from lovers and children to close networks of friends and business partnerships. The Ten brings a sense of perfect togetherness and achievement, and an appreciation of your place at home and in the wider world. An additional meaning is finding your ideal home.

REVERSED MEANING

The Ten reversed expresses the loosening of family ties and disruption to your social circle. Close friends move away—physically or emotionally—due to a development in their own lives which may leave a gap in yours. Consider that this card can arise if you are afraid of losing someone, and when there is a feeling of unrest due to something being taken from a family or group. This can manifest as a newcomer who brings an unwelcome influence.

TEN OF PENTACLES

UPRIGHT MEANING

The Ten of Pentacles in the upright position reveals inheritance, generosity, and possibly a love match that brings a wealth of love and happiness. The flavor of this card is also maturity, in terms of maturing investment policies, and also emotional wisdom. This is a time to enjoy the abundance of a family, and benefit from the shared resources and values that flow from one generation to the next.

REVERSED MEANING

Inevitably, the Ten reversed shows adversity concerning family money and property, and can reveal a love mismatch that is based on status rather than emotional bonds. There is a rigidity implied here too, where the expectations of older generations clash with those of younger members. The outcome is disconnection rather than dialog; values are not shared and money issues may become contentious.

TEN OF WANDS

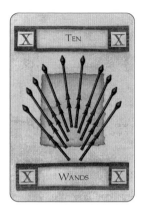

UPRIGHT MEANING

If the Ten of Wands is the first card to appear in a reading, you may want to reshuffle the deck and lay the cards again; the Ten is often a signal that you are overburdened and need to take more time in order to be receptive to the reading. The meaning of the Ten is that you are carrying the weight of the world, with all its attendant pressures. It is better to discard a little responsibly by choice, rather than drop all ten Wands because you cannot continue. The Ten may also indicate a burden of guilt.

REVERSED MEANING

The Ten of Wands reversed is a message that you need to lighten up, for the burdens that you carry are more imagined than actual. You may believe that others' demands on you are the sole cause of your predicament, but it may be easier to blame them than destroy the illusion of your own importance. When you stop diverting your energies to the needs of others, you will be able to care for yourself more effectively.

TEN OF SWORDS

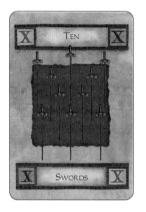

UPRIGHT MEANING

The Ten of Swords means sudden endings and change. It brings truth, and a release from uncertainty; you can see your situation exactly as it is. In work, this may mark the end of a relationship, job, or contract, and socially, a group may suffer discord to the extent that broken bonds seem irreparable. The message of this card is that there is nothing to do but accept this necessary conclusion.

REVERSED MEANING

In the reversed position, the meaning of the upright card stands. However, because more strife unfortunately may come, you may feel besieged by worry. The prospect of failure or conflict, however, is often more angst-ridden that the event itself; all you can focus on now is letting go. The world will turn, and you with it.

THE PAGES

THE PAGES OF the minor arcana are usually described as young people or children. However, their interpretation can be much more encompassing: the Pages are Peter Pans, so they include character types who are young at heart. Pages may be male or female; they are referred to as "he" or "she," but they are of course interchangeable.

Pages can also represent young situations, or new influences in your life. The type of influence is determined according to the element of each suit—emotional, idealistic, financial, or intellectual. Pages are messengers, bearing information; in this way they can be seen as transformational links, revealing how you get from one place in life to another. Like the Queens and Kings, Pages can also reveal aspects of our own personalities.

PAGE OF CUPS

UPRIGHT MEANING

The Page of Cups is a sociable, intuitive spirit who just loves good company and the good life. Traditionally, he is seen as sensitive and artistic: the archetypal creative dreamer (one interpretation is the psychic child). As a messenger, the Page has positive news about relationships and children. His presence can be reassuring, particularly if he arrives after a spell of emotional insecurity.

REVERSED MEANING

The reversed Page is a young person who is unable to express his feelings. He regresses to bouts of temper and tears and sulking to get the attention that he craves. The Page's message is fraught and possibly incomplete; you cannot get the whole story from this person, so in a reading, the card can show frustration and emotional blocks.

PAGE OF PENTACLES

UPRIGHT MEANING

The Page of Pentacles can be described as a hard-working, methodical young person. Reliable, willing to take responsibility for her actions, and dedicated to serving others, she brings good news about your financial affairs. This Page's appearance in your reading can also act as advice or a gentle warning: that a diligent attitude will help you to manage any existing or future financial pressures.

REVERSED MEANING

The Page reversed signifies mistrust. There is a fine line between theft and taking what she thinks she has a natural right to. This card reveals extravagance and irresponsibility. The Page's message here is that you may be restricted due to someone else taking too much away from you.

PAGE OF WANDS

UPRIGHT MEANING

The Wands bring conversations and conditions for success, so this Page is an inventive youth who is a natural communicator. As a message, the card says an offer is coming, and you will soon have news. The advice is to take this opportunity, but do check the details to ensure you understand exactly what is required.

REVERSED MEANING

The Page reversed can show a young person who is not communicative, and who may have difficulties with self-expression. When he makes an appearance in a reading, information is delayed rather than delivered. This card can also reveal deception through charm, and it is unlikely that promises will be kept. Beware offers that appear too good to be true.

PAGE OF SWORDS

UPRIGHT MEANING

Bright beyond her years, the Page of Swords has wit and perception. She brings good intelligence, along with helpful people who take swift action to help your cause. The Page's message is that you must rely on your brain to stay ahead. An additional meaning is signing documents.

REVERSED MEANING

The reversed Page is secret poison, manipulating people through misinformation and lies. As a go-between she stirs up trouble, and cannot be relied upon to be accurate about any arrangement. She may bring gossip and slander, which she circulates for her entertainment. Overall, the card in this position shows unfairness and poor judgement.

THE KNIGHTS

THE KNIGHTS ARE the seekers of the minor arcana, symbolizing action. The quality of this action depends upon the suit element. The Knight of Cups, with his element of Water, may prefer words and romantic ideals—a potential conflict with the traditionally martial role of Knight. The fiery, impulsive Knight of Wands is characterized by urgency and speed, but his influence may be fleeting as his interest burns bright, then burns out. The more placid Knight of Pentacles prefers to plod rather than race, while the Knight of Swords brings drama and battle.

KNIGHT OF CUPS

UPRIGHT MEANING

As Knights are action cards, an emotional Knight may not make the ideal companion. His appearance in a reading reveals a dreamy, affectionate individual who brings with him new friends for you. However, as a potential lover, he may not get around to demonstrating his intentions. His actions—or lack of them—may leave you confused. What is on offer? As a situation, the card can also simply mean an offer or proposal.

REVERSED MEANING

The negative traits of the upright Knight of Cups are magnified in the reversed position: this Knight cannot be trusted to keep a promise, turn up for an appointment, or acknowledge your feelings in any way. He may think, however, that he is being bohemian and romantic. As a broader situation, the card denotes disappointment.

KNIGHT OF PENTACLES

UPRIGHT MEANING

The Knight of Pentacles comes with a guarantee: travel with him and you get where you need to go. The journey ahead may not be exciting, however, but this steady, loyal character can be relied upon to make headway in business matters and find practical solutions to problems. Viewed as a situation, the upright Knight of Pentacles reveals that consistent effort will ensure progress, particularly in finance and education.

REVERSED MEANING

The Knight reversed pontificates, does little, and is dull. At best he is a ditherer, at worst a thief. When this card appears in a reading, it warns of financial impropriety and complacency. It is therefore best to play detective when dealing with any new financial advisors or institutions; naturally, make sure you check the small print of all policies and other contracts.

KNIGHT OF WANDS

UPRIGHT MEANING

The Knight of Wands is a passionate, liberal character who gets things moving; his irrepressible personality, however, can mean that he needs to indulge his dreams without others' input. As a situation, this Knight symbolizes a creative time during which decisions are made, and events speed up. Some readers say that the appearance of this card reveals a house move.

REVERSED MEANING

The Knight of Wands in the reversed position appears to make a contribution to an important project, but he is doing little except reveling in the attention that he gets from his new-found status. This card unfortunately reveals insincerity and apparent action, delay, and ensuing confusion. You may, therefore, need to protect yourself from an egotist. As a situation, the card advises caution.

KNIGHT OF SWORDS

UPRIGHT MEANING

As a personality, the Knight has drive and charisma, but he brings necessary battles that must be fought. Overall, this card can be interpreted as stressful situations—arguments, opposition, and outbursts. On a more positive note, this Knight, as a fast mover in a suit famed for action, represents a great surge of energy: events in your life speed up, and a drama unfolds.

REVERSED MEANING

The Knight of Swords reversed is a coward who does not do what he says he does. On the surface, he may appear to be forthright and confident; however, he has no courage or conviction. This Knight warns that someone whom you rely upon as an ally cannot be trusted to stay the distance. When interpreting him as a situation, the card often shows rivalry and feeling undermined.

THE QUEENS

TRADITIONALLY, THE Queens represent the influence of women; in a reading, the Queen can represent a partner, or she may symbolize aspects of the self. To identify her, one astrological technique is to consider the element of a Queen's suit and relate it to one of three possible Sun signs— for example, the Queen of Cups is ruled by Water, so she may reveal a mature woman born under the sign of Scorpio, Cancer, or Pisces (see page 22). The four Queens of the minor arcana can also be seen as four aspects of major arcana card III, the Empress: emotional and nurturing (Cups); creative and communicative (Wands); abundant and practical (Pentacles); and intelligent and protective (Swords).

QUEEN OF CUPS

UPRIGHT MEANING

The upright Queen of Cups is the Queen of Hearts: she represents love and natural beauty, and can symbolize the ideal partner. Sociable, sensitive, and artistic, her emotions rule her world. Faithful and nurturing, the Queen gives unconditionally to those around her. Intuition and perception are also highlighted when she appears, so this is a time to take note of your dreams. Within them, you may find hidden messages that help you follow your heart.

REVERSED MEANING

The Queen of Cups reversed is a competitive socialite who often thrives on other people's attention, yet she gives little in return. Her influence is draining and she is often envious. It is wise to take her seriously, as she is the Queen of broken hearts: her appearance in a reading can show deception and jealousy.

QUEEN OF PENTACLES

UPRIGHT MEANING

Generosity is the meaning of the upright Queen of Pentacles. She may appear as a mentor, in business or a family; this successful older woman has wisdom and funds at her disposal and uses them appropriately. In a reading, she represents generosity, and can also show feeling closely connected with animals and the natural world.

REVERSED MEANING

When reversed, this Queen uses money as a weapon with which to control others. She has little emotional literacy, and so expresses her insecurity through her spending patterns. Crashing between miserliness and extravagance, she brings a roller coaster of instability and is difficult to negotiate with. As a situation, she represents insecurity.

QUEEN OF WANDS

UPRIGHT MEANING

This Queen has a magic wand to ensure she gets her way. Sociable, forward-looking, and nurturing, the Queen of Wands reveals a woman who is in touch with her needs and ambitions. As a situation, she represents leadership, communication, and creative pursuits, such as acting and writing. As advice, you are asked to speak your truth.

REVERSED MEANING

The Queen of Wands reversed takes on more than she can handle. She is overprotective, and wants involvement in order to feel included. This, however, feels oppressive for those to whom she is closest. Her motivation may be pure, but what she says she can achieve is never demonstrated. As an influence, the card can show offers or help that do not materialize.

QUEEN OF SWORDS

UPRIGHT MEANING

This Queen is defined by her mental alacrity. Her company is stimulating and she uses her intelligence to entertain, enthrall, and challenge those around her. Forthright and graceful, she relies on logic and instinct to run her life. Her strength of character makes her a loyal friend, but in following true reason, she may tend to her own needs first before extending help to others. As an influence, she represents self-sufficiency.

REVERSED MEANING

The Queen reversed turns her sword on others, and may look for excuses to do so. Sharp-tongued to the point of brutality, she knows how to use words as a weapon. These are the actions of a bitter individual who may pose as a moralist. As a situation, this reversed card can show extreme defensiveness due to stress.

THE KINGS

TRADITIONALLY, the Kings represent the influence of a mature man; in a reading, the King can represent a partner; or he may symbolize aspects of the self. As with the Queens (see page 149), one identification technique is to consider the element of a King's suit and relate it to one of three possible Sun signs—for example, the King of Pentacles is ruled by Earth, so he may indicate a Taurean, Virgoan, or Capricorn man (see page 22). The Kings of the minor arcana can also be seen as four aspects of card IV, the Emperor, who represents order and rulership. When applying this to the suits, we get the following correspondences: mastery of emotions (Cups); creativity and impulse (Wands); loyalty and protection (Pentacles); intellect and action (Swords).

KING OF CUPS

UPRIGHT MEANING

The King of Cups has sensitivity. Kindly, reliable, and highly sociable, he follows his intuition when making decisions. As a master of emotions, at best he is sensitive to others' feelings; at worst he endeavors to overly control or suppress his own feelings, which makes him seem distant and difficult to pin down. His appearance in a reading signifies managing emotions, and problems solved.

REVERSED MEANING

The King of Cups reversed, unlike the upright King, shows feelings out of control. This can manifest in destructive behavior patterns, such as a refusal to discuss important issues or acting to disrupt a situation rather than manage it. He is emotionally vulnerable, and expresses this in an immature way.

KING OF PENTACLES

UPRIGHT MEANING

The King of Pentacles in the upright position shows pride in achievement. Often a professional or business owner, he works hard to protect and support those close to him. Generous and thoroughly reliable, he brings material comfort and practical support. As a predictive force, he heralds resolutions and reward.

REVERSED MEANING

The King of Pentacles reversed can be a dangerous opponent. It is important that he wins at all cost, and therefore is untrustworthy when dealing with any cause other than his own. Integrity and a good reputation are less important to him than immediate gain. This King can foreshadow debt and insecurity, particularly regarding property matters. An alternative reading of the card is workaholism.

KING OF WANDS

UPRIGHT MEANING

The King of Wands has entrepreneurial spirit, a traveler who loves exploration and freedom. He is protective, but he understands others' needs to express themselves as individuals. This gives him a maturity and wisdom that naturally attracts respect. As an influence, the card shows friendship, communication, and charisma.

REVERSED MEANING

The King reversed has a narrow mindset. As his upright twin comprehends the need for a free spirit, so this negative ruler is a strict disciplinarian. He is the overbearing father or boss, but here tinged with bitterness or bigotry. As a situation, the King can reveal resentment and egotism.

KING OF SWORDS

UPRIGHT MEANING

The King of Swords is a master of the mind; he relies on his wits, and his influence and ambition are clear. Willing to fight for the prize, he is comfortable in conflict and will not flinch when challenged. He makes fast decisions, and as a situation shows final outcomes, such as legal judgements, and the need for strategy and planning. In relationships, the card can reveal a lack of understanding and emotional distance.

REVERSED MEANING

The King of Swords reversed represents dangerous opposition. He wields his sword ruthlessly and his mind-games may be relentless. When he appears in a reading, you may be dealing with someone who will try to outwit you in any way he can, playing a cruel game of cat and mouse. It may be best to retreat rather than continue to fight with him.

Tarot Resources

Bibliography

Tarot: The Open Reading, Yoav Ben-Dov (CreateSpace, 2013)

The Magic of Tarot, Liz Dean (CICO Books, 2019)

Tarot: An Illustrated Guide, Jonathan Dee (D & S Books, 2000)

The Tarot, Alfred Douglas (Penguin, 1988)

Sasha Fenton's Fortune Telling by Tarot Cards, Sasha Fenton (Zambezi Publishing, 2002)

The Complete Illustrated Guide to Tarot, Rachel Pollack (Element Books, 1999)

The Pictorial Key to the Tarot, Arthur Edward Waite (Samuel Weiser, Inc., 2000)

A History of Playing Cards, Roger Tilley (Studio Vista, 1973)

The Tarot: Art, Mysticism, and Divination, Sylvie Simon (Alpine Fine Arts Collection, 1986)

The Encyclopedia of Tarot (Vol. I), Stuart R. Kaplan (U.S. Games Systems, Inc., 2001)

The Complete Book of Tarot, Juliet Sharman-Burke (Pan Books, 1985)

Initiation into the Tarot, Naomi Ozaniec (Watkins Publishing, 2002)

Cards

The Visconti-Sforza Tarot is a generic term referring to a number of editions of the Tarots painted for the Visconti and Sforza families. These decks are usually dated between 1428 and 1450 and are named after the collections in which they are presently held. The three principal Visconti-Sforza Tarots are the Pierpont Morgan-Bergamo (presented throughout this volume); the Cary Yale, and the Brera. Some Tarot scholars believe that these decks were painted to commemorate important dates in the history of the families, such as the wedding of Filippo Visconti and Maria de Savoy in 1428; the marriage of Bianca-Maria Visconti and Francesco Sforza in 1441; and 1450, when Francesco Sforza was crowned Duke of Milan. There is much debate over which deck commemorated which occasion. For further reading on this, I highly recommend Stuart R. Kaplan's *Encyclopedia of Tarot*, Volume I, as listed in the bibliography above.

To obtain the Visconti Tarot and the other Lo Scarabeo decks reproduced in this volume, contact: www.loscarabeo.com

Author website
www.lizdean.info

Picture Credits

PAGE 1: Justice, Visconti Tarots, Lo Scarabeo Edizioni D'Arte.

PAGE 2: *Top left*: the Chariot; *top right*: the Fool; *below left*: the Emperor; *below right*: Strength, all from the Visconti Tarots, Lo Scarabeo Edizioni D'Arte.

PAGE 3: Judgement, Liguria-Piedmont Tarot, Lo Scarabeo Edizioni D'Arte.

PAGE 5: Detail from the Moon, Oswald Wirth Tarot, Bridgeman Art Library.

PAGE 6: The Sun, Classic Tarot, Lo Scarabeo Edizioni D'Arte.

PAGE 7: Cloud card from the Dante Tarot, Lo Scarabeo Edizioni D'Arte.

PAGE 8: Justice, Charles VI (Gringonneur) Tarot, Bridgeman Art Library.

PAGE 9: The High Priestess, Visconti Tarots, Lo Scarabeo Edizioni D'Arte.

PAGE 10: The Fool, Tarot of Marseilles, Mary Evans Picture Library.

PAGE 11: The Crocodile, Grand Tarot Belline, Bridgeman Art Library.

PAGE 12: The Magician, Visconti Tarots, Lo Scarabeo Edizioni D'Arte.

PAGE 13: *Left*: the Knight of Cups, Visconti Tarots, Lo Scarabeo Edizioni D'Arte; *right*: the Knight of Swords, Tarot of Marseilles, Mary Evans Picture Library.

PAGE 14: The Ace of Swords, Liguria-Piedmont Tarot, Lo Scarabeo Edizioni D'Arte.

PAGE 15: The Ace of Cups, Guildhall Library, London.

PAGE 16: From the Egyptian Tarot, Lo Scarabeo Edizioni D'Arte.

PAGE 17: The Moon, the Tarot of the Sphinx, Lo Scarabeo Edizioni D'Arte.

PAGE 18: The Chariot, Oswald Wirth Tarot, Mary Evans Picture Library.

PAGE 19: *Left*: Judgement, copyright 2002 Beth Moon—all rights reserved; *right*: the Lovers, Rider Waite Smith Tarot, Bridgeman Art Library.

PAGE 20: The Ace of Coins, Minchiate Florentine, Lo Scarabeo Edizioni D'Arte.

PAGE 21: The Emperor, Minchiate Florentine, Lo Scarabeo Edizioni D'Arte.

PAGE 23: *From left to right*: the Star, the Sun, and the Moon, Visconti Tarots, Lo Scarabeo Edizioni D'Arte.

PAGES 24, 25: The Fool and the Tower, Etteilla Spanish Tarot, Bridgeman Art Library.

PAGE 26: From the Tree of Life Tarot, Urania Verlag AG Müller.

PAGE 28: Detail of the Hermit, Oswald Wirth Tarot, Mary Evans Picture Library.

PAGE 29: *Top*: detail of the Moon, Rider Waite Smith Tarot, Bridgeman Art Library; *center*: detail of the Knight of Swords, Tarot of Marseilles, Mary Evans Picture Library; *bottom*: detail of Strength, Visconti Tarots, Lo Scarabeo Edizioni D'Arte.

PAGE 30: Detail of the Moon, Oswald Wirth Tarot, Bridgeman Art Library.

PAGE 31: *Top*: detail of Temperance; *center right*: detail of the Empress; *left*: detail of the High Priestess, all from the Visconti Tarots, Lo Scarabeo Edizioni D'Arte.

PAGE 32: The Queen of Coins, Tarot of Marseilles, Mary Evans Picture Library.

PAGE 33: *Left*: the Two of Coins, Zigeuner Tarot, Urania Verlag AG Müller; *right*: the Star, Crystal Tarot, Lo Scarabeo Edizioni D'Arte.

PAGE 34: From the I Ching of Love, Lo Scarabeo Edizioni D'Arte.

PAGE 60: *Left*: the Tower; *center*: the World; *right*: the Moon, all from the Visconti Tarots, Lo Scarabeo Edizioni D'Arte.

PAGES 66, 68, 70, 72, 74, 76, 78, 80, 82, 84, 86, 88, 90, 92, 94, 96, 98, 100, 102, 104, 106, 108: major arcana from the Visconti Tarots, Lo Scarabeo Edizioni D'Arte.

PAGE 111: The Ace of Cups, Tarot of Marseilles, Mary Evans Picture Library.

PAGE 113: The Ace of Cups, Visconti Tarots, Lo Scarabeo Edizioni D'Arte.

PAGE 116: The Two of Swords, Visconti Tarots, Lo Scarabeo Edizioni D'Arte.

PAGE 119: The Three of Coins, Visconti Tarots, Lo Scarabeo Edizioni D'Arte.

PAGE 122: The Four of Wands, Visconti Tarots, Lo Scarabeo Edizioni D'Arte.

PAGE 125: The Five of Cups, Visconti Tarots, Lo Scarabeo Edizioni D'Arte.

PAGE 128: The Six of Swords, Visconti Tarots, Lo Scarabeo Edizioni D'Arte.

PAGE 131: The Seven of Coins, Visconti Tarots, Lo Scarabeo Edizioni D'Arte.

PAGE 134: The Eight of Cups, Visconti Tarots, Lo Scarabeo Edizioni D'Arte.

PAGE 137: The Nine of Wands, Visconti Tarots, Lo Scarabeo Edizioni D'Arte.

PAGE 140: The Ten of Coins, Visconti Tarots, Lo Scarabeo Edizioni D'Arte.

PAGE 143: The Page of Wands, Visconti Tarots, Lo Scarabeo Edizioni D'Arte.

PAGE 146: The Knight of Cups, Visconti Tarots, Lo Scarabeo Edizioni D'Arte.

PAGE 149: The Queen of Swords, Visconti Tarots, Lo Scarabeo Edizioni D'Arte.

PAGE 152: The King of Coins, Visconti Tarots, Lo Scarabeo Edizioni D'Arte.

PAGES 22, 35–59, 61, 62, 63, 65, 67, 69, 71, 73, 75, 77, 79, 81, 83, 85, 87, 89, 91, 93, 95, 97, 99, 101, 103, 105, 107, 109, 114-115, 117-118, 120-121, 123–124, 126–127, 129–130, 132–133, 135–136, 138–139, 141–142, 144–145, 147–148, 150–151, 153–154: cards illustrated by Emma Garner from *The Magic of Tarot* (book and Tarot deck) by Liz Dean, © CICO Books.

Art
Hebrew letter art on pages 24, 25, and 27 by Samantha Wilson.
Aleph card on page 27 by Mandy Pritty.

Particular thanks go to Sasha Fenton and the late Jonathan Dee for their help in sourcing Tarot cards.

INDEX

Page numbers in *italics* refer to captions

ACKNOWLEDGMENTS

With thanks to all at CICO Books, and to David Fordham for his creative design.